Geopolitics, Security and Bilateral Relations–

Perspectives From India and South Korea

Geopolitics, Security and Bilateral Relations— Perspectives From India and South Korea

Edited by

Maj Gen BK Sharma (Retd)

and

Cdr MH Rajesh

(Established 1870)

United Service Institution of India

New Delhi (India)

A RINSA–USI Joint Research Initiative

Vij Books India Pvt Ltd
New Delhi (India)

First Published in India in 2017

Published by

Vij Books India Pvt Ltd
(Publishers, Distributors & Importers)
2/19, Ansari Road
Delhi – 110 002
Phones: 91-11-43596460, 91-11-47340674
Fax: 91-11-47340674
e-mail: vijbooks@rediffmail.com
web : www.vijbooks.com

Copyright © 2017, United Service Institution of India, New Delhi

ISBN: 978-93-85563-83-6 (HB)

ISBN: 978-93-85563-84-3 (ebook)

Contents

Preface   vii

Introduction – by *RINSA*   1

Chapters

1. Emerging Geopolitical Trends in East Asia   5

    Seok-soo Lee

2. Geopolitical Trends in Indo-Pacific: Implications For
    Regional Security   21

    Maj Gen B K Sharma

3. Cooperative Governance in East Asia: Lessons from
    European Case   37

    Hanbeom Jeong

4. Security Cooperation between Republics of India
    and Korea   51

    Lalit Kapur

5. Nuclear Security Issues: Challenges and Opportunities
    (North Korea's Nuclear Threat Perspective)   68

    Yong Soo Kwon

6. Nuclear Security Issues: Challenges and Opportunities   85

    Dr Roshan Khanijo

7.   Bilateral Cooperation between the ROK and India:
     ROK's Perspective   103

     Park Min-hyoung

8.   India South Korea Relations — An Indian Perspective   123

     MH Rajesh

Conclusion – by *USI*   138

Index   143

Preface

In a significant step, during Prime Minister Narendra Modi's visit to South Korea in 2015, India and the Republic of South Korea (RoK), scaled up their bilateral relations to the status of *'special strategic partnership'*. A year before that, in 2014 the South Korean Prime Minister Park Geun-hye, was the Chief Guest at the annual Republic Day Parade in New Delhi. The relationship, since then, has grown substantially. Keeping this perspective, the two premier think tanks namely United Service Institution of India (USI) from India and Research Institute for National Security Affairs (RINSA) of Korea National Defence University, Republic of South Korea decided to partner each other to enhance and define the major contours of this bilateral relationship through a joint research project. This book owes its genesis to that decision.

Historically, legend has it that thousands of years ago, Queen Suriratna or Hur Hwang-ok came to Korea from Ayodhya, a historical place in India, This relationship continued during the Buddhist era. Thus the cordial relationship built in the past is continuing and has in fact become more pronounced through the upgradation to 'Special Strategic Partnership'. The changing dynamics post-Cold War brought India and South Korea further close, as liberalization of Indian economy allowed the Korean value chain to invest westwards, and India became a major stopover and a manufacturing hub for the Koreans. Culture followed commerce and the Korean music and serials become a rave in India, (as a part of the global phenomenon of the Korean *'Halyu'* wave). Thus a very cordial relationship developed between the two countries which benefitted them immensely.

It is in such a backdrop that United Service Institution of India (USI) and Research Institute on National Security Affairs (RINSA) collaborated on a joint research project namely "Geopolitics, Security and Bilateral Relations: Perspective from India and South Korea". Four scholars each from USI and RINSA conducted research on subjects of mutual interest. Given the emerging strategic partnership between India and South Korea, they were tasked to address domains ranging from geopolitics of the regions, bilateral relations, to security cooperation and nuclear issues. The main purpose was to enhance mutual understanding about the newly emerging security environment and examine strategic challenges and opportunities.

The result, are the eight papers published in this book, which I am sure will give readers, both the Indian and South Korean perspectives on matters, relevant to the geo-strategic environment, particularly the Indo-Pacific region and the security concerns, especially the nuclear challenges. Considering both India and South Korea are surrounded by nations who have the proclivity to escalate tensions through lowering the nuclear thresholds, it becomes important to analyse the nuclear dynamics. In addition, approaches to enhance the bilateral relations through expanding economic interactions and political communications were also deliberated. It is hoped, that this book will serve as the starting point to further engagements and research on the subjects which are of importance to both the countries.

Lt Gen PK Singh (Retd)
Director
United Service Institution of India
New Delhi

Introduction

– *RINSA*

Since India and South Korea established a diplomatic relationship in 1973, the bilateral relations continue to grow across sectors. It is evolved to 'strategic partnership.' Seoul and New-Delhi shares values and interests in several aspects. First of all, India is the largest democracy in the World, while South Korea achieved democratization in a relatively short period. Both countries adopted market economy as an economic system. It is these commonalities that lay the groundwork for bilateral cooperation. With shared political and economic system, they pursue same national objectives of prosperity and security, which are intertwined. Same systems and common interests provide rationales for close collaboration between the two players.

Bilateral economic cooperation demonstrated a good performance over the decades in trade and investment. India appreciates South Korea which boldly took risk to invest in India, which had a bleak prospect of economic success in the early 1990s. South Korea also appreciates India for providing opportunities for expanding market vice versa. On the basis of economic achievement, the two states wanted to expand cooperation to political and defence area. Security cooperation has been included in the seven agreements concluded at the recent summit in Seoul. In an MOU, both sides promised to establish a new communication channel between the National Security Council Secretariat of India and the Office of National Security of South Korea.

Along with accumulated bilateral relations over decades, changing security environment at regional and global level drives cooperation between the two middle powers included in G20. Recently, the term of 'Indo-Pacific' increasingly gained currency among pundits and policy-makers. In the past, Asia-Pacific and East Asia were more popular in defining geographical scope of strategic discussion. Two developments uphold the Indo-Pacific as an emerging regional security construct. With the trends of geopolitics changing rapidly, the dynamics of regional players are transformed. There is no doubt that geopolitics is largely defined by great powers' rivalry between the United States and China. Their competition is understood as a product of China's rise. Amid increasing tension between the rivalries, growing India became more active and influential player. Prime Minister proclaimed that 'Look East' policy should be replaced by an 'Act East' one during his official visit to Seoul in May 2015.

Even if South Korea remains preoccupied by Northeast Asia, it considers a broader scope of issues in the region for strategic and economic purposes. During the Cold War, Northeast Asia is its primary concern because it occupied the center of strategic gravity, significantly affecting the destiny of the divided Korea. With dramatic transformation of geopolitics following the end of the Cold War, a unipolar system led by the United States was built and a Pax-America seemed realized. Various initiatives for multilateral security cooperation covering the Asia-Pacific were mainly presented by Canada and Australia. It is this circumstance that induces experts to use the Asia-Pacific confines. Then, East Asia was employed to effectively discuss multilateral security cooperation led by ASEAN. For instance, East Asia Summit was created in 2005.

The Indo-Pacific concept began to receive attention from expert of the Asia-Pacific. There emerged a strategic assessment by South Korean experts that India could take an expanded role for peace and stability in the region. Yet, Seoul shows no serious concern over security in Indian Ocean. In this vein, South Korea remains worried about the usefulness of the broad region for strategic discussion, while recognizing the advent of the Indo-Pacific era. The main reason is that South Korea confronts military threats from North Korea, which conducted nuclear test four times with enormous conventional capabilities. Preoccupation with North Korea's threats kept South Korea from widening geographical definition of the region.

In these bilateral and regional contexts, it is even more pressing to bolster the strategic partnership between the two countries by improving political and defence communication, expanding economic interactions, and enhancing mutual cultural understanding. It is timely for USI (India) and RINSA (South Korea) to conduct a joint project on India-South Korea security cooperation. This is the first joint effort between the two prestigious institutes to do research together on security issues. The primary purpose of the joint work is to enhance mutual understanding of newly emerging security environment in the region. Secondly, the project examines strategic challenges and opportunities posed by a transition of geopolitics. Lastly, the co-work is devoted to draw approaches and measures to facilitate regional security cooperation and bilateral relations between India and South Korea.

The project is predicated on a couple of assumptions. Firstly, the regional scope is broadened to the Indo-Pacific. Secondly, India's overall national might continue to be strengthened and its role expanded. Thirdly, South Korea as a middle power, wants to be part of regional security rearrangement. Lastly, India and South Korea share interests and values and urgent need to bolster bilateral relations. With the research purposes and fundamental assumptions, the two institutes convened workshops in Seoul and New-Delhi. Through the two workshops, participants in the project exchanged ideas, perspectives and assessments in order to prepare a coordinated edited book as a final product of the joint work.

This publication consists of four main parts. Two experts from India and South Korea address either similar or same topic in each part. It could be helpful for readers to draw similarities and differences by making comparison of both articles. Part I is description and assessment of shifting regional geo-politics, presenting threat perceptions by India and South Korea.

In terms of scope, the former is broader than the latter. Part II is discussions on comprehensive security arrangements. The part introduced Indian and Korean perspectives. Part III deals with nuclear security issues, combining Indian and Korean analyses. Part IV focuses on bilateral cooperation between Korea and India.

As mentioned, Korea and India could collaborate in planning and implementing the path for moving the bilateral relations forward. In future studies, the RINSA and USI could play a significant role in designing roadmaps for India-Korea cooperation. The first work we carried out could lay the cornerstone for more detailed future studies. A temporal agreement after the joint work is that the cooperation could serve peace, prosperity, and human dignity of the two countries and the region as a whole.

Chapter One

Emerging Geopolitical Trends in East Asia

Seok-soo Lee
(Director-General, the RINSA, South Korea)

Introduction

East Asia remained peaceful since the end of the Cold War mainly due to strategic leadership by the United States in the region. However with a rising China, East Asia witnessed the realignment of regional geopolitics.[1] The United States tries to maintain and strengthen US-dominant order in the region, while growing China challenges the status quo forged by the United States. Attempts have been made to reconfigure power distribution in the region by a growing China. The escalating tensions in the South China Sea highlight a standoff between the United States and China.

Termination of the bloc politics at the global level brought about a uni-polar strategic framework in East Asia.[2] Given the uni-polar international system, the United States stayed dominant in East Asia as the only superpower. The absence of a competing peer ensures US-led regional security environment for a while. The seemingly fixed regional construct became unstable by the advent of a strong China equipped with economic and military might. With onset of the current decade, existing power distribution underwent modification in East Asia.

Peaceful development is the primary national objective of China. In order to achieve that goal, China wants to maintain favourable relations with the United States and other regional countries. But China became aggressive and assertive to the extent that it could not tolerate any thing that affects its core interests such as territorial sovereignty, security, and development. Furthermore, the tension between China and Japan has been on the rise due to several reasons such as military confrontation, difference in interpretation of history, and the rise of nationalism in both countries. The accelerating rift between the two countries resulted in territorial dispute in the East China Sea.

Economic growth of China nudged China's ambition to be a powerhouse in the region. Resources available to her have been mobilized by Beijing for the elevation of regional and global status. Military and economic instruments are used to gain leverage to other regional states. For instance, ASEAN member states are heavily relying on trade with and investment by China, while they are increasingly dependent on the United States militarily. They are worried of China's aggressiveness and assertiveness in the South China Sea. Because of economic interdependence, regional countries would like to have better relations with China. But China's strategic expansion to the South China Sea poses military threat to ASEAN countries.

Confronting China's rise, the United States sought an option to effectively deal with a new geopolitical reality and ensure peace and stability in the region. For the United States, regional security and economic success seems to be a product of the long-lasting U.S. primacy in East Asia. In order to maintain a predominant position, Washington announced a new regional strategy of 'pivot' and rebalance to the Asia-Pacific region. The strategy led to a reallocation of overseas military capabilities of the U.S. in favour of the Asia-Pacific region. Given the financial difficulty, the United States has tried to bolster alliance and improve relations with friends and partners in the region. In other words, the U.S. military build-up has been complemented by enhanced cooperation with allies and partners.

This paper is mainly designed to trace the changing nature of geopolitics in East Asia as a product of China's ascent. A basic assumption of the study is that the major power rivalry between the United States and China is a source of turbulence in strategic landscape in East Asia.

The paper consists of three parts. First of all, it describes the emerging trend of geopolitics in the region. Then, it explores contributing factors to the geopolitical change. Last part is devoted to a discussion on both implications of a new geopolitics for regional peace and stability and how to successfully convert competition and confrontation to cooperation and accommodation among regional actors.

I   Emerging Geopolitics in East Asia

China's rapid economic growth gave rise to the increase of military expenditure. As a result, China continued to modernize military capabilities especially in the area of navy, which are closely associated with power projection in East Asia. The regional policies by China were directed at the United States and regional countries. On the basis of overall growing power, China wanted to have a new relationship with the United States. Commencing 2010s, Chinese leaders, Hu Jintao and Xi Jinping stressed that it was necessary to establish a new type of major power relations for regional peace and stability. China's assessment is that the United States put priority to its interests first and ignored China's interests in the past. For shaping a constructive relationship, Beijing asked Washington to acknowledge the status of China as the world's 2nd largest economy and its major concerns and core interests.

Further, it is contended by China that the two major powers should forge a new relationship to avoid war. China warned that armed clash could take place between the rising power and an existing hegemon. According to a Beijing's proposal, a new relationship should be embodied by 'reciprocal' and 'equal' relations, which could be conducive to conflict avoidance, mutual respect and a win-win relation. China repeatedly stressed that both countries should mutually admit core interests and major concerns, while arguing that it has respected those of the United States without exception but the United States did not reciprocate. Sovereignty, security and economic development constitute the core interests of China. China frequently mentioned and reiterated the new relations between the two major countries with an intention to elevate its global status and extending its influence in East Asia.

With its status elevated by a new type of major power relations, China intends to induce neighbors to take side with it. Diplomatic, economic and military assets were utilized by China for the better relations with Southeast Countries. Economic abundance formulates a foundation of coercive diplomacy to ASEAN countries. For instance, economic assistance has been provided to selected countries such as Cambodia, Laos and Myanmar. Trade and investment also play a crucial role in broadening China's realm of influence in the region.

Among others, China's military build-up significantly affects neighboring countries' attitudes and behavior to China. Power projection capabilities constitute the main source of threat abroad. As China grows stronger, East Asian countries feel strategically trapped between the United States and China in any sense. Given a certain security condition, a country could be forced to make choice between the two major powers. Dispute in South China Sea is one case. Countries involved in the dispute are Taiwan, Brunei, Malaysia, Indonesia, Philippine, and Vietnam, including China. Reclamation is in process in this area by China and Vietnam. Philippine and Vietnam have been in acute dispute with China.

In response to China's rise and its growing dominance in the region, the United States adopted 'rebalance' to the Asia-Pacific strategy. The rebalance strategy originated from a vision of "America's Pacific Century" presented by State Secretary Hillary Clinton in October 2011. Secretary Clinton offered an idea of strategic turn to the Asia-Pacific region.[3] Following Clinton, President Barack Obama mentioned U.S. efforts to advance security, prosperity and human dignity across the Asia-Pacific in November, 2011.[4] The term 'rebalance' was first used in the Defence Strategic Guidance (DSG) by the Department of Defence in 2012.[5]

In the beginning, the rebalance to the Asia-Pacific region was military-oriented, representing modest realignment of military capabilities. The DSG used 'rebalance' in the context of a major defence-resource shift, stressing the two components of the rebalance: relationships with Asian allies and key partners; an underlying balance of military capability and presence.[6] Since the end of 2012, the United

States began to emphasize diplomatic and economic aspects of the strategy. This change rests on the judgment that military approach cannot effectively address challenges from a rising China and a comprehensive approach is required.

With the rebalance adopted as a regional strategy, the United States has been cautious and hesitant to accept China's suggestion for a new model of superpower relations. Several considerations affected the U.S. reaction to the proposal. First of all, it is difficult for the United States to acknowledge China's core interest as sovereignty issues in disputed areas. Secondly, Washington has a different approach to form a new relation with Beijing. While the former took case by a case approach, the latter wanted a planned and systemic one. The United States wants China to assume responsibilities for global challenges, not completely recognizing China's core interests. Last but not least, it is afraid of sending the wrong signal to allies and partners which could perceive waning U.S. It also worries about a dramatic change of established status-quo in the region.

President Xi's recent visit to the United States clearly shows opportunities and limitations of the two big powers relations.[7] The two leaders addressed global issues including Afghanistan, peacekeeping, nuclear security, wildlife trafficking, ocean conservation, sustainable development, food security, public health and health security, humanitarian assistance and disaster responses and multilateral institutions. They also touched on bilateral relations comprising Confidence Building Measures (CBMs), cyber-security, counter-terrorism, and people to people exchange. The two big powers demonstrated common interests in and concern over global agenda, while showing limitations in dealing with bilateral issues. For instance, they made no progress on the territorial disputes in the South China Sea, which is one of China's core interests. It is proved at the summit that it called on China to take responsibilities on global issues but rejected advancing a new relationship with China.

As examined, strategic landscape has been shaped by the two world's leading powers at the regional level. Within the framework of China-U.S. relations, other countries have had interactions with the two dominant powers. Regional countries can be categorized into three groups: pro-U.S.; pro-China; and neutral groups. The difficulty of classification lies in the fact that relations can vary across sectors. Most of states in the region shares economic interests with China, while most of them rely on U.S. presence and role in the region for security. Regional views of the U.S. rebalance imply relations between the United States and regional countries in security area. As figure shows, the U.S. allies are strong supporters of the balance, while China, North Korea and Russia are of negative attitudes to the rebalance.

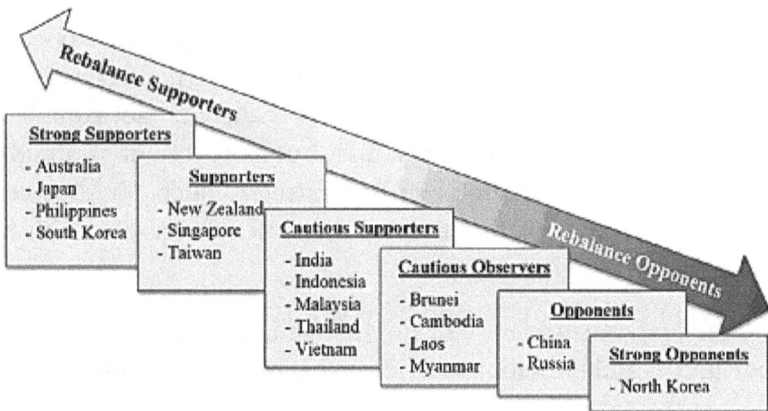

Source: David J. Berteau, Michael J. Green and Zack Cooper, *Assessing the Asia-Pacific Rebalance*, CSIS, December 2014, p. 20.

Strategic tension has been on the rise as China became aggressive and assertive on territorial disputes since an incident in 2010 in the waters near the disputed Senkaku/Diaoyu islands.[8] Furthermore, Beijing's claims over disputed islands in the South China Sea have raised tension and threatened regional stability. The South China Sea became a flash point in East Asia. North Korea's nuclear program could be a game changer in the region, raising concerns over a nuclear proliferation in Northeast Asia. North Korea did not listen to even China's recommendations for denuclearization and conducted nuclear test four times.

II   Determinants of Regional Geopolitics

At the center of a newly emerging security structure are, among other factors, China's rise and an ensuing power transition defined by shifting regional balance of power.[9] China's economic growth is an engine of military build-up in China. Between 1998 and 2007, China recorded an average annual economic growth rate of 12.5%.[10] In 2015, China allocated $145 billion to defence budget in comparison with about $10 billion in 1997.[11] This trend reveals a huge increase of military spending less than a decade. With boosting defence spending, China continued to pursue military modernization to build robust military capabilities. China's modernization efforts appear comprehensive, systemic, and well-planned.

Despite a rapid military build-up, China remains much weaker than the United States in terms of aggregate military power.[12] The United States has the largest military budget in the world which is bigger than combination of following big military spenders of China, France, UK, Japan and India. It is world number one in terms of defence budget, weapon systems, research and development, training and education and experience of war. It maintains overall military superiority even in East Asia. Meanwhile, Chinese forces are far inferior to their U.S. counterparts in quality of equipment, experience and training.[13]

Even though it is observed that China reduced the disparity with the United States in military capabilities, China remains limited in various aspects. China still suffers from underdeveloped power projection capabilities and deficiency in training and operational abilities.[14] Despite recent advance in power projection capabilities, the operational range is not much extended due to limited number of small tanker aircraft that could refuel aircraft in the air during fighting.[15] PLA revealed shortcomings in air and naval operations at a distance from mainland. For training, China's armed forces never had combat experience since its border conflict with Vietnam starting 1979.

An estimate indicates that the overall U.S. military might have experienced degradation due to under investment, poor implementation of modernization program and budget sequestration on readiness and capacity.[16]According to a Heritage report, the United States' military posture is rated as 'marginal' and in trending toward 'weak.'[17] Given the trend of U.S. military shrinking and rapid military modernization by PLA, the gap of military capabilities between the major powers is getting gradually narrowed. It is, however, widely accepted that there is a long way to go for China to be equivalent to the U.S. military capabilities.

Apart from aggregated military might, geography and distance matter.[18] A recent dynamic study shows that the location of the battlefield affects regional power balance.[19] Strategic advantages and disadvantages can be meaningfully determined by the location of operational area. In sum, China has more advantages in the areas close to mainland. For instance, it maintains strategic edge in Taiwan Strait rather than South China Sea because of operational distance. Geographical advantages help China challenge the United States and its allies and partners more seriously.

Balance of the aggregated military power could lead to misunderstanding of East Asia security construct. Also, a static counting of overall manpower and equipment cannot capture a power balance between major powers in operational context of battlefields.

It would be wrong to underestimate China's military capacities on the basis of overall military power which could inflict damage to the United State forces in East Asia. It is the shifting military balance across flash points that drive a new military competition between the two leading powers in the region. As such, superpowers' rivalry defines a new trend of geostrategic landscape in the region.

Interdependence among regional countries plays a role in shaping security conditions in East Asia. First of all, the extent of interdependence should be examined between the United States and China. Interdependence has intensified between the two big countries across various areas such as trade, China's holding of U.S. debt, information technology and cyber-risk, energy and people to people exchanges.[20] Trade and educational exchanges promote cooperation and mutual understanding, while the effects of interdependence in other issues are in question. Pundits point to both negative and positive impact on the bilateral relations between the two leading countries with military and economic power.[21]

Economic interactions also influence security environment in East Asia. There has been a myth that economic interdependence contributes to regional peace and stability. Emerging China-centered economic order make us rethink the correlation between security and interdependence. The problem is that interdependence in East Asia is by nature asymmetric. Due to China's rapid economic growth, small countries became more dependent on China. As a result, China expanded its clout to neighbors in the region. A dichotomous structure appeared: China-centered economic activities; and the U.S.-centered security arrangement.[22]

With regard to the effect of interdependence on geo-politics in East Asia, there are two contending arguments. Traditionalists focus on its positive impact on peace and stability, while revisionists stress its negative impact on security dynamics. Growing economic leverage of China could make small countries feel threatened by a coercive diplomacy of China with economic instruments. With China's influence threatening neighbors, small and middle countries became more dependent on the United States for security. In this line of reasoning, interdependence does not necessarily bring about cooperation and strategic stability.

Middle powers in the region play a growing role in ensuring peace and stability in East Asia. Here, middle countries involve South Korea, India, Japan, Indonesia and Australia, which show commonalities and differences. South Korea, Japan and Australia are strong allies of the United States. South Korea moved relations with China forward for the purpose of economy and security. Economically China is the topmost trade partner to South Korea. Seoul needs Beijing's help in dealing with North Korea's nuclear and missile program. Japan has acutely confronted China on the basis of a robust alliance with the United States, expanding its military activities.

While maintaining a neutral position in foreign policy, India wants to play a constructive role to promote regional peace and prosperity.

South Asia is a new engine for growth. Australia is also active in making contribution to establishing rules and orders in the region. Indonesia with the largest population in Southeast Asia has been eagerly pursuing economic development. For India and Indonesia, peaceful and stable environment is prerequisite for prosperity. A group of middle powers could affect forging cooperative security configuration in East Asia.[23] Middle powers are in general concerned over peace initiatives, which are designed to facilitate multilateral security cooperation.

Various non-state actors have been increasingly involved in relations in East Asia.[24] They can be categorized into benign and malign group. The former includes MNCs (multinational corporations), the UN, World Bank, the IMF, EU, and others, while the latter comprises terrorist groups, pirates, drug-dealers and so on. For example, terrorist attacks could pose threat to the regional stability. While multilateral organization for economy and security could make contribution to regional security, diversification of non-state actors could bring either positive or negative impacts on the region.

Along with material base of relations, ideational factors of perceptions and identities could lead to misunderstanding and distrust in East Asia. First of all, interpretation of history caused conflicts among neighboring countries. South Korea and Japan showed divergence in understanding of history specifically during the colonial rule. This is the case between China and Japan too. Mobilizing nationalism is greatly effective in bolstering popularity for domestic politics. Nationalistic sentiment could trigger conflict among nations. Then, regional actors, for instance, share value of innovation, market and meritocracy. Furthermore, they should abide by international order and law. These ideational commonalities could contribute to the region in the two directions: conflict and cooperation.

The North Korean nuclear development could affect the bilateral relations between the two big countries. China's policy of North Korea's nuclear build-up could provide either an opportunity or a challenge to U.S.- China cooperation. The United States has wanted China to punish North Korea harshly, severing all sort of economic assistance especially including oil. China joined sanctions taken by the

UN Security Council but it fell short of the U.S. and South Korea's expectation. Even though recent debate centers round the question of whether Pyongyang is a strategic asset or liability, Beijing seems to not give up North Korea for security reasons. It is observed that China continues to treat North Korea as an ally and a buffer zone. China's lukewarm response to North Korea's nuclear test could increase a tension between the United States and China, while a close policy coordination to dismantle North Korea's nuclear program could promote cooperation.

Given changing trends of security dynamics, East Asia witnessed broadening and deepening of security concept. The two major powers stressed comprehensive components of security consisting of traditional state to state military threats and non-traditional transnational ones. The latter provides cooperative agenda. Regional cooperation could be enhanced by dealing with non-traditional security issues such as terrorism, global health, climate change, environment, international crimes, piracy, and energy.[25] In addition, deepening of security concept help actors promote regional cooperation rather than confrontation and competition. East Asian countries are increasingly concerned over global and regional security. This deepening trend could contribute to stable regional arrangement.

III   Implications for Regional Security

The new trends of geopolitics indicate growing tension and destabilization of East Asia with the potential for accommodation. It is proved that security configuration is attributed to redistribution of power, interdependence, roles of middle powers, growing number of non-state actors, ideational factors, North Korean nuclear development program, and broadening and deepening of security concept. Redistribution of power plays a decisive role in shaping security environment. Other factors are associated with cooperation and conflict as well. Their impacts on geopolitics, however, seem to be limited at best.

Security environment in East Asia appears uncertain and complex. At this moment, there is no doubt that confrontation prevails over accommodation in a geostrategic sense. A major powers' rivalry is the case in point. Given confrontation between the two major powers, there is little room for middle and small countries to take a middle path between the two. In the meantime, East Asia has accumulated experience of regional cooperation especially since the end of the Cold War. All in all, a new strategic confrontation poses challenge to the regional security, while amassed practice of cooperation provides an opportunity to the region.

While engaging in competition, the United States and China makes substantial efforts to promote cooperation at bilateral and multilateral levels. The U.S.- China Strategic and Economic Dialogue is an annual high-level meeting to discuss a wide range of regional and global strategic and economic issues between both countries. Even if military competition grows, shared interests could drive their collaboration on military security issues. Mutual confidence has been boosted by active communication, military exchange programs and joint exercises. Easing tension between the two powers is a prerequisite for peace and stability in East Asia.

To reduce lingering bilateral animosity and accrued confrontation, multilateral efforts should be made. Diverse multilateral formats were created for more stable and resilient security environment in East Asia. Member countries of ASEAN played a leading role in promoting multilateralism in the region.[26] As a result, there are various multilateral venues for cooperation such as ARF (ASEAN Regional Forum), APT (ASEAN Plus Three), EAS (East Asia Summit), ADMM+ (ASEAN Defence Ministers Meeting Plus), APEC (Asia-Pacific Economic Cooperation), ASEM (Asia-Europe Meeting), CSCAP (Council for Security Cooperation in the Asia Pacific), Shangri-La Dialogue, Six-Party Talks, and others. Almost all regional actors joined more than one of these arrangements.

It is a widespread criticism that they lack efficiency, coordination, and strong leaders. In addition, the preoccupation with soft security issues points to another limitation that existing architectures failed to collaboratively deal with military security problems. Weakness of existing architectures indicates that unlike Europe, an effective and integrated framework with a strong leadership could not be easily established in East Asia. Given roadblocks to multilateralism, overcoming these shortcomings is an enduring task. One of recommendations is that rising middle powers of India, South Korea, Indonesia and Australia should make contribution to enhancing multilateral cooperation.

As India pursues rapid economic growth as a primary national goal, regional stability and cooperation is desperately required. As exports began to forge a crucial portion of economy, maritime security is essential to India's economic development. Furthermore, India is the world's largest democracy, and is growing stronger. It is increasingly interested in becoming a global power strong enough to contribute to preserving a liberal, rules-based international order.[27] Against this backdrop, India looms as a leading country in the Indo-Pacific as a whole. Since India has maintained good relations with big, middle, and small regional actors under the principle of non-alignment, it could play a productive role of enhancing amity and cooperation and reducing hostility and confrontation.

Australia has shown concerns over multilateral security cooperation since the end of the Cold War. Given alliance with the United States, it has made much effort to establish cooperative security mechanism in the region. Further it is highly sensitive to rule-based international order.

Since the late 1980s, Seoul has enthusiastically pursued diplomacy for multilateral security cooperation: Roh Tae-woo' proposal for a six-party Consultative Conference for Northeast Asia; Kim Dae-jung's East Asian community; Lee Myung-bak's New Asia Initiative; and Park's Northeast Asian Peace and Cooperation Initiative (NAPCI). The initiative proposes an incremental approach in establishing a security framework, placing focus on such soft security issues as disaster relief, nuclear safety, environmental protection, public health, energy security, cyberspace security, and transnational crime. In a following stage, the expected framework could address hard security issues. President Park's drive for security mechanism in Northeast Asia could precipitate cooperation, gradually diminishing tensions in the region.

Endnotes

1   "Geopolitics is discourse about world politics, with a particular emphasis on state competition and the geographical dimensions of power," cited from *Global Asia*, Vol. 9, No. 3 (Fall 2014), p. 11.

2   East Asia includes Northeast Asia and Southeast Asia. When geo-politics is discussed, geographical scope matters. The scope of debate reflects the nature of shifting regional strategic arrangement. Recent studies tend to expand regional scope to Indo-pacific. This paper adopts the term of East Asia that seems to be more relevant in discussing geopolitics from South Korean perspective.

3   Hillary Clinton, "America's Pacific Century,"*Foreign Policy*, October 11, 2011, http://www.foreignpolicy, com/2011/10/11/americas_pacific_century, accessed on December 1, 2015

4   Barack Obama, "Remarks by President Obama to the Australian Parliament" (speech delivered to the Australian Parliament, Canberra, Australia, November 17, 2011), http//www.whitehouse.gov/the-press-office/2011/11/17/remarks-president-obama-australian-parliament, accessed on December 1.

5   U.S. Department of Defence, *Sustaining U.S. Global Leadership: Priorities for 21ˢᵗ Century Defence* (Washington, DC: U.S. Department of Defence, January 2012), 2, http://www.defence.gov/news/defence_strategic_guidancel.pdf.

6   David J. Berteau, Michael J. Green and Zack Cooper, *Assessing the Asia-Pacific Rebalance*, CSIS, December 2014, p. 4.

7   White House, Fact Sheet: President Xi Jinping's State Visti to the United States, September 25, 2015, https://www.whitehouse.gov/the-press-office/2015/09/25/fact-sheet-president-Xi-jingping, accessed on December 2, 2015.

8   Chinese fishing boat and Japanese Coastguard ships collided on September 7, 2010. Chinese captain of fishing boat was arrested and detained for about two weeks.

9   By Oystein Tunsjo, "The Cold War as a Guide to the Risk of War in East Asia," *Global Asia*, Vol. 9, No. 3 (Fall 2014), p.16, "While other factors contribute to explaining China's growing assertiveness in recent years, systemic shifts in the distribution of capabilities and the transition to a US-China bipolar international system are the major factors accounting for increased tension and conflict in maritime East Asia."

10 Richard A Bitzinger, "China's Double-digit Defence Growth," *Foreign Affairs* (March 19, 2015), p. 1, https://www.foreignaffairs.com/print/1113889, accessed on December 4, 2015.

11 Ibid., p. 1

12 In the 2016 state of the Union Address, President Obama declared that "the United States of America is the most powerful nation on Earth. It's not even close. We spend more on our military than the next eight nations combined. Our troops are the finest fighting force in the history of the world." See http://www.whitehousegov/blog/2016/01/12, accessed on January 16, 2016.

13 Thomas J. Christensen, "China's Military Might: First, the Good News," *Bloomberg View*, June 4, 2015, http://www.bloomberview.com/articles/2015-06-04/china-s-militry-might-first, accessed on December 2, 2015.

14 "Geography critical factor in U.S.-China rivalry," Interview with Eric Heginbotham, *Korea Herald*, December 2, 2015, http://www.koreaherald.com/common_prog/newsprint.php?ud=20151202001097&dt=2, assessed on December 4.

15 Ibid.

16 The Heritage Foundation, *2016 Index of U.S. Military Strength*, p. 12.

17 Ibid.

18 "Geography critical factor in U.S.-China rivalry," Interview with Heginbotham; Thomas J. Christensen, "China's Military Might: First, the Good News": Eric Heginbotham and et al., *The U.S.-China Military Scorecard: Forces, Geography, and the Evolving Balance of Power 1996-2017* (Santa Monica, Calif.: RAND, 2015)

19 Heginbotham and et al., *The U.S.-China Military Scorecard: Forces, Geography, and the Evolving Balance of Power 1996-2017*, xix-xxxi.

20 Trade volume is increasing. The United States imported $125 billion of goods from China and $425.5 billion in 2012. The United States is the most favourable destination for Chinese students who want to study abroad.

21 Thomas Wright, "Sifting through Interdependence," *The Washington Quarterly*, 36:4 (Fall 2013), pp. 9-14.

22 Ibid., p. 14.

23 For more discussion, see Jan Melissen and Yul Sohn, "Leveraging Middle Power Public Diplomacy in East Asian International Relations," *EAI (the East Asia Institute) Issue Briefing* (November 24, 2015)

24 Carder broadly pointed to three groups of non-state actors: the sub-national (local NGO and municipal actors); the trans-national (an association of big city leaders

and multinational cooperation), the supra-national (EU, IMF, World Bank, and the UN), See, Kent E. Calder, "The Traps of Geopolitical Discourse and the Mandate for New Thinking," *Global Asia*, Vol. 9, No. 3 (Fall 2014), pp. 58-62,

25 The United States treats terrorism, climate change, global health as security threat, in The White House, *National Security Strategy*, February 2015; China defines comprehensive security as including traditional threats and non-traditional ones (terrorism, transnational crimes, environment security, cyber security, energy and resource security and major natural disasters. In Xi Jinping, "New Asian Concept for New Progress in Security Cooperation," Remarks at the Fourth Summit of the Conference on Interaction and Confidence Building Measures in Asia, Shanghai Expo Center, 21 May 2014

26 The term of ASEAN centrality highlights its central role in framing and enhancing multilateral security cooperation in East Asia.

27 David Feith, "The U.S.-India Strategic Test," *The Wall Street Journal*, December 4-6, 2015.

Chapter Two

Geopolitical Trends in Indo-Pacific: Implications For Regional Security

Maj Gen B K Sharma

*"In this century, the Asia- Pacific and the Indian Ocean
Rim which some now refer to as the Indo-Pacific will
become the world's center of gravity."*

Former Australian Defence Minister Stephen Smith.

Introduction

The term Indo-Pacific has a recent origin, which combines Indian Ocean and Pacific Ocean. Australia's Defence White Paper, 2013[1] alludes, 'Indo-Pacific' means "multifaceted globalization has ensured that developments from the Suez Canal to the Sea of Japan or from African shores of the Indian Ocean to the western Pacific were strongly interrelated and mutually dependent". The emergence of this newly defined area is termed by some observers as an "Indo-Pacific Pivot."[2] The region encompasses almost half of the world population, three of ten largest economies, more than fifth of world GDP, 1/3 of world exports and half of the world's maritime tonnage. It is home to an enormously populous and diverse mix of ethnicities, cultures, political systems, religions and economies. The region is the maritime trade highway of the world and combines Southeast Asian states with the western Pacific, functioning as the throat of sea routes punctuated by Strait of Malacca, Sunda, Lambok and Makassar. Across the ASEAN archipelago Ocean Region (IOR) is a critical hub for trade and energy transfers. At least 40 per cent of the world's sea ocean borne trade, 50 percent of its container traffic and 70 percent of the traffic in hydro-carbon products transits through the region. Almost 68 percent of India's, 80 percent of China's and 25 percent of the US' oil is shipped from the IOR. Uninterrupted flow of oil, natural resources and goods is extremely crucial for developing economies, like India and China.

The geopolitics in the Indo-Pacific Region (IPR) is characterized by competition for domination of strategic resources and locations, freedom of navigation, and arms race, including nuclear proliferation. Coupled with these are the challenges of rising spectre of non-traditional threat. If the stakeholders are unable to manage the competition, the region would lend itself to conflicts over border and maritime disputes, ethno-religious fault lines, nuclear brinkmanship, etc leading to aggressive military posturing. Ultra-nationalism and strategic mistrust displayed by contestants are the contributory factors that maximize chances of conflict. However, on the positive side, shared economic prospects offer hope for cooperation and trans-border non-traditional threats are incentives for building cooperative security.

Strategic Trends

Quest for Balance of Power. The Indo-Pacific region is the center of gravity of global power shift. While the US seeks to maintain a status quo in the world order and international system, China, on the other hand, asserts for recognition as a major power and strives to carve out its own sphere of influence. The regional countries are on the throes of a dilemma of how to balance between the two competing protagonists. Robert Kaplan argues that in the absence of credible US military presence in the region, there is a risk of China "Finlandising" smaller countries and going to war with Japan over Senkaku/Diaoyu islands.[3] Apart from the US and China, Russia, India and the ASEAN countries too are seeking balance of power in Indo-Pacific, which are detailed in the succeeding paragraphs.

US Asia-Pivot (Rebalancing) Strategy

"After a decade in which we fought two wars that cost us dearly, in blood and treasure, the United States is turning our attention to the vast potential of the Asia Pacific region...from the Pacific to the Indian Ocean...the United States of America is all in[4]."

– Barack Obama, 17 November 2011.

Kenneth Lieberthal, articulates views on American Pivot to Asia in an article publish by Foreign Policy Issue-21 Dec 2011[5]. Perusal of this article and plethora of literature on the point to following understanding of the enunciated strategy:-

➢ The Pivot to Asia strategy is marked by six guidelines; strengthening bilateral security alliances, deepening relationship with emerging powers including China and Vietnam, engaging with multilateral institutions, expanding trade and investment, forging a broad-based military presence, and advancing democracy and human rights. Treaty alliances with Japan, South Korea, Australia, Philippines and Thailand are noted as the fulcrum of strategic turn to the Indo-Pacific reforms.

➢ The operational part of the strategy envisages setting up of innovative rotational deployments of self-sustaining forces, designation of military force to IPR, allocation of 60% of the air force resources, including tactical aircraft and bomber forces from the continental US and similar percentage of its space and cyber capabilities besides deployment of 60% of naval assets in the Western Pacific and Indian Ocean. A number of bare-bones diversionary airfields are developed in the Indo-Pacific for flexible deployment of aerospace assets as part of Anti-Access Area-Denial (A2AD) counter measures. Some US military thinkers speak about a 'Hub and Spoke[6]' military strategy that envisages using Guam in the Pacific Ocean and Diego Garcia in the Indian Ocean as the two hubs and the operating bases in the rim of two oceans as spokes to deal with China militarily.

➢ In June 2013, Defence Secretary Chuck Hagel at the Shangri-La Dialogue stated that the US will not let sequestration affect Asia Pivot strategy. US has further strengthened its defence relations with Australia and Japan. The possibility of quadrilateral strategic partnership between the US-India-Japan-Australia is being explored from time to time to provide traction to Pivot to Asia strategy.

➢ However, escalating conflict scenarios in the West Asia, Ukraine and Af-Pak region are posing multiple challenges to the US to combat expansionist designs of ISIS/ Al-Qaeda /Taliban on the one hand and of Russia and China on the other. These new challenges will have unintended consequence for prosecution of Asia Rebalancing Strategy'.

China's Counter Intervention Strategy

"Profound changes are taking shape in the Asia-Pacific strategic landscape. Relevant major powers are increasing their strategic investment. The United States is reinforcing its regional military alliances, and increasing its involvement in regional security affairs."

"People's Republic of China, National Defence White Paper 2010.[7]

➢ China's 'Counter Intervention Strategy' is aimed at countering the US rebalance to Asia, preventing the formation of anti-China coalition on its periphery, and weakening US alliances. To achieve this, China is pursuing three core security objectives in East Asia: exerting control over its 'near seas'; promoting China-centered regional economic integration; and defending and advancing Chinese sovereignty claims in South China Sea (SCS).

➢ China considers western Pacific vital for its sovereignty, integrity, security and development. For geographically restrained China, the security of coastal economic centers of gravity, access to energy, raw materials, export markets and security of SLOCs is critical. The PLA- Navy (PLAN) counter–piracy missions in the Gulf of Aden and its much-debated 'Malacca Dilemma' underscores the seriousness of Beijing's security concerns along this route. Therefore, in China's security calculus, SCS assumes great strategic importance. In 2006, President Hu Jintao described the PRC as 'a great maritime power' and urged the transformation of navy from 'near seas active defence' (first group of islands i.e. Kuril-Ryukyu-Taiwan-Philippines-Brunei) to 'far sea defence', second group of islands (Japan, GUAM, northwest Pacific Ocean and even the Indian Ocean). [8] In order to bolster its maritime claims in SCS it has embarked upon a major drive of reclamation of reefs and shoals and is developing military infrastructure on artificially created islands.

➢ China's 'Silk Road Economic Belt and 21st-Century Maritime Silk Road' (Belt and Road Strategy) on the lines of the ancient Silk Road, aims at increasing connectivity in the region and selling the dream of "enabling everyone to share development opportunities."

➢ China's asymmetric warfare capability has achieved a moderate level of sophistication. China's hi-tech enabled navy and air force, offensive cyber warfare capability (espionage and sabotage), anti-satellite weapons, assured second strike nuclear capability and 'Assassin's Mace' weapons have lend credibility to its 'Anti-Access Area-Denial' (A2-AD) strategy against the US led intervention forces.

➢ In May 2014, during the CICA (The Conference on Interaction and Confidence-Building Measures in Asia) at Shanghai, President Xi Jinping added another proposal by unveiling 'New Asian Security Concept'. The so-called 'New Security' concept envisages a combined security based on shared destiny, shared interests and shared benefits.

➢ China is deliberating confidence-building measures with stakeholders in East China Sea (ECS) and SCS, but disfavours involvement of outside powers (USA) in regional disputes. China has often emphasized that good-neighbourly policy does not mean compromising on disputes over sovereignty, territory, and jurisdiction. China believes that growing Chinese economic and military clout will over time persuade its neighbours that there is more to gain from accommodating Chinese interests than from challenging them.

Russia's Pivot to East Asia. The strategic community is debating over Russia's so called 'Pivot to East Asia'. President of Russia in his speech at the APEC underscored the strategic outlook of his country in these words, "In sheer geopolitical terms, landmass, natural resources and military capabilities, Russia remains a major power in the region. It also sits in close proximity of many key countries in Asia-Pacific".[9] Development of energy rich Eastern Siberia and the Russian Far-east and its integration with northeast Asia as a common energy grid remains the main strategic economic goal. Russia seeks to diversify its energy export markets by supplying energy to regional economic powers and capitalize thriving container trade in the region. Russia's traditional interests in East Asia have intensified by its closer relationship with Vietnam, South Korea, Japan and India. The $400-billion, 30-year natural gas deal signed by China and Russia in May 2014, signaled a major and sharp turn for its economic and strategic focus to Asia. Russia's 'pivot to Asia' and dramatically enhanced relations with China; will have substantial long-term implications for Asia and more broadly for the IPR. Conduct of Sino-Russia military exercises in the Pacific Ocean is a regular event. Geopolitics of Arctic and Northern Sea Routes (NSR) will add another dimension to strategic competition in the region.

India's Act East Policy. India's geostrategic location and rising politico-economic profile provides it a competitive strategic advantage in the IOR. India's Act East policy[10], initiated in 1991, represents its efforts to cultivate extensive economic and strategic relations with Southeast Asia to bolster its standing as a regional power and a counterweight to Chinese strategic influence. The policy has supported India's economic transformation and growth, enabled development of its lagging regions (particularly the seven north-eastern states), and is helping India to shape an Asian economic community. India's 'Act East Policy' seeks inter-alia engagement of East Asia and the Pacific Region. India supports the creation of a Pan-Asian Free Trade Area (FTA), comprehensive economic cooperation, collective security of SLOCs as well as critical infrastructure and cyberspace and collaborative measures against non-traditional threats. India strongly advocates amicable resolution of inter-state disputes and a sound climate change strategy. Engagement with China, and a close strategic relationship with US and other countries will remain the cornerstones of its 'Act East Policy'. High level visits to Japan, Myanmar, Australia and Fiji in 2014 and Singapore, China, Mongolia, South Korea and Bangladesh in 2015 are pointers of Indian initiatives to add teeth to this policy. India seeks a free and just world order, wherein among other things, it has access to global common resources and markets and freedom of navigation in the international waters.

ASEAN Rebalancing in East Asia and Southeast Asia. ASEAN[11] brought coherence to a region of enormous political and economic differences. However, the great power rivalry in the region is widening the division in the ten-member grouping. Broadly, those members with claims in SCS, want ASEAN to register serious concerns over what they see as China's belligerent actions to enforce its claims in the waters of SCS and over the Spratly, Parcel and other islands and atolls. However, non-claimants, mainly Cambodia supported by Laos and Myanmar, are reluctant to alienate China. They align with China's position on dealing with the issue on bilateral basis. China, as one writer puts it, may have obtained an "outsider's veto" over ASEAN when its interests are threatened[12]. China sees no role of ASEAN in territorial disputes with other member states. ASEAN seems to be caught between a rising China on the one hand and a freshly engaged US, seeking to balance against China, on the other.

Sovereignties Issues. China and Taiwan claim 80% of the SCS based on "Nine dashed line". The contested areas include Paracel islands, occupied by China but claimed by Vietnam: and Spratly Islands disputed by China, Taiwan, Philippines, Malaysia, and Brunei. In the ECS, similar disputes occur between Japan and China over the ownership of Senkaku / Diaoyao, between South Korea-Japan over Dokdo/

Takeshima islands and between Russia and Japan over Kurile Islands. Disputes in the SCS and ECS can disrupt the sea-borne trade and dampen economic prosperity. The stand offs between Chinese vessels with US naval ships and fishing boats and energy vessels of Philippines and Vietnam, declaration of Air Defence Identification Zones (ADIZ) and exclusive maritime zones heighten security challenges and risk of conflict. A politico-economically fragile North Korea, with propensity to use military force and flex nuclear muscle, further aggravates the risk of confrontation.

Indian Ocean Region. China's "Far Seas Ocean Strategy", is aimed at inter alia safeguarding its interests in the IOR. In PLAN's definition "Far Seas" area stretches from the Northwest Pacific to the East Coast of Indian Ocean and beyond to the East Coast Africa. The strategic competition in the IOR is heating up. From Xinjiang, China is developing an economic corridor to Pakistan. The project entails development of Gwadar in the Arabian Sea as a petro-chemical hub and construction of Karakoram overland bridge, across Khunjerab pass to Kashgar in Xinjiang. Another strategic transportation corridor being developed by China is from Myanmar to Kunming. The strategic transportation corridor from Kyaukpyu comprising, rail-road-energy-pipelines-runs to Kunming. China is advocating multilateral BCIM (Bangladesh- China-India Myanmar) corridor to connect to South Asia. Kyaukpyu (Bay of Bengal) in Myanmar has been developed into another petro-chemical hub with facilities for super tankers to discharge crude. In China's perception, IOR is the arena where India-US-Japan strategic interests coalesce and present a formidable threat to Chinese SLOCs, the very lifeline of China's economy. The recent port calls by PLAN conventional submarines in Karachi and Sri Lanka as well as reported forays of PLAN nuclear- powered submarines into IOR are harbingers of China's increased military interest in the region. Indian Ocean, due to its vast resources, huge market, sea lines of communication (SLOCs) and unstable countries has gained importance for all the major powers. More than 120 extra-regional warships are present here throughout the year. USA maintains a forward naval posture using bases in Diego Garcia and the Persian Gulf, both to deal with fragile security scenarios in the Middle East and to keep other states from gaining influence in this key area. It aims to protect the SLOCs, prevent any blockage to oil flow from the Gulf region and also create what China, increasingly competing with USA for regional influence, perceives as a threat to its energy security, described by some as its 'Malacca Dilemma'. India has applied soft power by becoming a major foreign investor in regional mining, oil, gas and infrastructure projects. India has also spread its influence across the entire IOR, through trade and investment, diplomacy and strategic partnerships. PM Modi's recent visits to Seychelles, Maldives Sri Lanka, Mozambique and Bangladesh are an indication of addressing China's strategic challenge in India's backyard. Analysts are of view that if China, USA and India do not constructively engage each other, the IOR will end up as an ocean of conflict and turmoil.

West Asia Quagmire. Energy rich Middle East continues to be in a state of strategic flux due to intra state conflicts and possibility of inter-state conflicts. Sectarian strife manifest in Sunni-Shia divide is the principle driver of emerging conflict between Iran and Saudi Arabia, both vying for regional leadership. Its new manifestation is the Yemen Crisis, where Iran backed Houthis is in severe conflict with Saudi backed leadership. Iran - Shia ruled Iraq -Assad regime in Syria-Hamas and Hezbollah aligned on one side and Saudi Arabia, Sunni world and US led west on the other side have set the stage for a wider divide in the Muslim world. The Sunni-Shia sectarian violence has the potential to spread to Pakistan and Afghanistan. Israel's military response to these security developments remains unpredictable. The overall security scenario in the Middle East is fraught with high security risks of intra and inter-state conflicts that would be potentially damaging for trade and energy flow in the Indo-Pacific Region[13].

South Asia. The region now faces far more virulent form of hybrid threats that combine asymmetric conflicts with conventional wars, under a nuclear overhang. The vexed nature of Indo–Pak and Sino-India border disputes has led to wars in the past. Contested sovereignty therefore continues to be a flash point for future conflicts. The nature of border disputes is more complicated in Ladakh, with contention over Siachen glacier, Shaksgam Valley[14] and presence of Chinese in the Northern Areas of Pakistan Occupied Kashmir (POK). In Kashmir and

Ladakh region, strategic objectives of China and Pakistan converge. Kashmir and boundary issue will continue to bedevil Indo-Pak relations. Water security dominates Pakistan's security concerns vis a vis India. China, on the other hand, is building dams over Brahmaputra River that causes concerns in India and Bangladesh. Border and water disputes, terrorism and vexed India-Pakistan-China relations therefore would continue to pose a major security challenge in the region.

Economic Competition and Cooperation.

> The US seeks to benefit from the economic dynamism of the region. It has signed Free Trade Agreements with various countries including, Singapore Australia and South Korea. The lynchpin of US economic rebalancing is the Trans-Pacific Partnership (TPP) - an economic bloc comprising 11 countries, namely US, Chile, New Zealand, Brunei, Singapore, Australia, Peru, Vietnam, Malaysia, Mexico and Canada. With the inclusion of Japan and South Korea in the TPP[15] in the future, it would have a combined GDP of $ 26 trillion i.e., about 40 % of global GDP and over 30 percent of world exports.

> Another competing economic bloc is Regional Comprehensive Economic Partnership (RCEP). It is a Free Trade Agreement (FTA) scheme of the 10 ASEAN Member States and its FTA Partners (Australia, China, India, Japan, Korea and New Zealand) to be concluded by the end of 2015. It includes more than 3 billion people, has a combined GDP of about $17 trillion, and accounts for about 40 percent of world trade. China is an important economy of RCEP[16].

> China also has set out to alter the global financial structure with its banks and fund initiatives that have accompanied the Silk Road Idea. The Asian Infrastructure Investment Bank (AIIB) and the Silk Road Fund which are Chinese Initiatives, New Development Bank (NDB) which is a BRICs initiative have begun the process. Several US allies have joined AIIB, when Japan and US has steadfastly refused indicates a brewing financial polarization. The current slowdown of Chinese

economy has serious implications for global trade, reduction in imports of raw materials and export of goods besides sparking off a social unrest in China.

➤ Presently bulk of global trade is conducted in U.S. dollars and more than 60 percent of all global foreign exchange reserves are held in U.S. dollars. The factors such as the US heavy international debtor and China as the second largest economy in the world have sparked a growing discussion among policy makers and academics that the world should no longer rely on a single, dominant currency, such as the dollar. China has just entered into a very large currency swap agreement with the Eurozone that is considered a huge step toward establishing the Yuan as a major world currency. China is the largest producer and one of the largest importers of gold in the world. Experts believe that China eventually plans to back the Yuan with gold and try to make it the number one alternative to the U.S. dollar. In 2010, a joint study was undertaken by Asian Development Bank and Columbia University's the Earth Institute inferred that Yuan can become alternate reserve currency[17].

Security Challenges

The overwhelming geostrategic importance of the IPR notwithstanding, the region faces a myriad of security challenges explained below.

(a) **Arms Race.** As per the Military Balance 2014, published by the International Institute of Strategic Studies (IISS), since 2014, there has been a constant increase in defence spending in Southeast Asia (6 %) which is the highest in entire Asia[18]. North Korea has continued with its nuclear tests. Experts are of the view that North Korea's Unha series satellite launch programme, which saw its first successful test trial in Dec 2012 from Sohae Space station, has reached a rudimentary level of launching an ICBM with a payload. Japan is the third largest defence spender in Asia ($ 51 billion) as per IISS Military Balance 2014. Japan's Defence Policy Programme-2012, underscored the need for a dynamic transformation of its Defence Forces, from basic defence to offensive defence capability, to protect it's off shore island territories. Abe's idea of amending 'Article Nine' of the constitution that precludes formation of a regular army is gaining traction. A panel report recommended that the country's "Self Defence Forces"(SDF) be allowed to act more like a normal army[19]. The other countries too are augmenting their coastal defence and maritime surveillance capability-with preference for acquisition of submarines and modern naval platforms.

(b) **Nuclear Proliferation.** Declared weapon states like India, Pakistan, and North Korea are constantly improving their nuclear weapons, whereas, there has been a respite in Iran with the deal[20]. Israel, known to have breakout nuclear weapon capability, is showing no signs of capping their nuke ambitions. Perceived nuclear threat from North Korea has made Japan open the debate about its nuclear option, especially if the American policy of extended deterrence changes, reports of South Korea's demand to develop a reprocessing plant are indicators that nuclear issue has the potentiality to become active if there is a change in the geo-strategic alignment. North Korea has conducted three tests thus far, has plutonium stock for half a dozen bombs. Miniaturizing the nuclear warhead is an ongoing process. Similarly, in West Asia, Saudi Arabia is debating about acquiring nuclear weapons considering the imminent threat arising from Iran and Israel, on the other hand, the other gulf nations are trying to acquire "Missile Defence" from the US. Pakistan has deployed Tactical Nuclear Weapons (TNWs) and is developing sea-based nuclear weapons capability. Its declared policy of 'First use' and emerging nuclear capabilities have lowered the nuclear threshold and increased the risk of nuclear conformation in South Asia.

Non-Traditional Security Challenges

Terrorism: Rise of ISIS in the Middle East is the biggest challenge faced in the IPR. ISIS continues to hold ground in Iraq and Syria. More than 4 million refugees have fled ISIS ruled areas in Syria, while most of them have gone to Turkey and Lebanon, a significant number have come to Iraq, placing pressure on local services and infrastructure. Iran proxies Hizbollah and Hamas too remain a formidable terrorist threat in Middle East. Terrorist organizations in Africa include Boko Haram, Al Shabaab and Al Maghrib. Af-Pak region has infamously come to be known as an epicenter of international terrorism. Pakistan-Saudi Arabia- US created Frankenstein monster is now fully grown and is out of control. Al Qaeda –Taliban and its affiliates are enthused with rabid Wahabi-Salafi ideology and profess notion of creating Emirates and Caliphates. In the Pacific, prominent terrorist threats include Abu Sayyaf in Philippines and Jemaah Islamiyah in Indonesia.

IPR landscape is witnessing pronounced nature of asymmetric threats. Drug trafficking, proliferation of WMD, cyber security, nuclear terrorism piracy and migrations are other challenges that undermine humanitarian security. The IPR is also beset with rising sea-levels, Tsunami, nuclear disasters, piracy and pandemics. The ungoverned spaces and fragile states are being dominated by non-state actors spreading radical ideologies and using disruptive technologies to threatens humanity security. The crises in the West Asia poses a major trans-regional security threat whereas the growing Islamist radicalization in South Asia poses a risk of state collapse in Pakistan & Afghanistan and instability of Central Asia. Asymmetric nature of warfare is strongly eroding the efficacy of conventional military capabilities to deal with emerging security threats.

Implications for Regional Security. There are a number of flashpoints in the region between China-Japan, China-Vietnam and South Korea-North Korea in Asia Pacific. The issues of contested sovereignty have the potential to trigger a big crisis while nuclear North Korea could trigger a conflict with South Korea. These issues could embroil the US in these conflicts. West Asia remains one of the most unstable regions in the world. There is Shia-Sunni divide in the region while it remains unclear how the Iran-Israel rift would shape up after the US-Iran nuclear deal. Rise of the ISIS as a transnational threat is the biggest challenge faced by the region. South Asia remains the epicenter of terrorism in the world and links between ISIS and Af-Pak terror groups could trigger a bigger crisis in the already fragile region.

Pakistan continues to use terrorism as a state policy to undermine India's conventional military advantage and draw attention of international community towards Kashmir issue. There is possibility of limited India Pakistan war under a nuclear overhang in the region. India-Pakistan and India-China border disputes remain flashpoints in the trouble India-Pakistan-China triangle. Military and nuclear nexus between Pakistan and China intends to achieve a blue water navy leading to strategic brinkmanship between India and China in the IOR. There are non-traditional security threats as well in IOR, like rising sea level, climate change, disaster management, cyber security.

Way Forward

There is urgent need to harmonize functioning of regional organisations in Asia Pacific - APEC (Economic Cooperation), ARF (Security Cooperation) & EAS East Asia Summit (Multi- Disciplinary), TPP, RCEP. China and the US should work closely on N. Korea under Six-Party Talks. The scope of DoC should be expanded to include freeze on up- gradation of military structures in the disputed areas while a Joint Working Group (JWG) should be established to discuss security issues. Planned military exercises should be notified well in advance. Efforts should be made to establish hotlines between Defence Ministries of claimant countries to report and manage untoward incidents. Claimants should also sign agreements on prevention of incidents at sea among themselves. There is should be absolute transparency in military modernization programs by publishing White Papers and dialogue at various regional forums. Creation of regional cooperation framework agreements for combating non-traditional security threats would lead to trust building in the region. In the Middle East, there is a need for an international coalition under the aegis of UN to tackle the IS. There is an urgent need to moderate Pakistan's behavior by the international community for stopping state sponsored cross border terrorism against India. Afghanistan needs continued international engagement for security and economic stability. SCO, CSTO and BRICS should explore ways to increase their profile in Afghanistan. There is need for a collaborative security arrangement to fight terrorism while strategic trust building should be undertaken in IOR through alternative security architecture and strategic dialogue between the stakeholders.

Endnotes

1 http://en.wikipedia.org/wiki/Indo-Pacific

2 http://thediplomat.com/2013/09/30/india-and-the-rise-of-the-indo-pacific/

3 Kaplan Robert, "The Gift of American Power," stratfor, 14 May , 2014.

4 Obama, Remarks by President Obama to the Australian Parliament.

5 Kenneth Lieberthal, "The American Pivot to Asia: Foreign Policy ", 21 Dec 2011.

6 Lee Jashyon, " Pac Net#57- China recreating the American Hub and Spoke System" , CSIS, Sep 9, 2015.

7 Chinese Communist Party, China's National Defence in 2010, 31 March 2011, Information Office of the State Council, available at <http://www.china.org.cn/government/whitepaper/node_7114675.htm>, accessed 7 May 2012

8 Clarke Ryan, "Report on Chinese Energy Security and the Role of the PLAN", Culture Mandala: Bulletin of the Centre for East-West Cultural & Economic Studies, Vol. 8, Issue 2, December 2009, pp.1-19.

9 Putin, "Asia Pacific Key to Russia's Future", APEC, 2012.

10 Prashanth Parameshwaran, " India's Vice President on ASEAN Voyage to Indonesia, Brunei", Diplomat, October 29, 2015

11 The Economist, "The Banyan, Getting in the way", 17 May 2014.

12 Park Chan Thul and Martin Petty (2012), " Analysis : China's sway over Cambodia tests Southeast Asian Unity", August 12.

13 The future of Sea Lane Security between the Middle East and Southeast Asia (2015), Chatham House Report.

14 Manoj Joshi (2015), " Why India insists on keeping Gilgit Baltistan Firmly in the Kashmir Equation," The Wire.

15 Overview of the TPP, Office of the US Trade Representative Website.

16 Wikipedia RCEP page.

17 Reuters (2010), " Yuan can became alternative reserve currency to US dollar – ADB". June 2014

18 Military Balance 2014.

19 The Economist, " Japan and America Closer Allies", May, 17, 2014.

20 Jack Kim & Ju-Min Park (2015), " North Korea says main nuclear complex operational, warns US," Routers, Sep 2015.

Chapter Three

Cooperative Governance in East Asia: Lessons from European Case

Hanbeom Jeong

(Korea National Defence University)

Abstract:-The interest in cooperative governance in security area is growing because the concept of security has extended in its content and range. The meaning of security is getting comprehensive including non-traditional threats such as economic crisis, human rights violations, terrors, environmental issues, maritime security, natural disaster, etc. The discussions on cooperative governance are heating up in East Asia, especially in Northeast Asia because this region has faced various security challenges for several decades. European case of multilateral security cooperation, especially OSCE (CSCE), provides a role model of cooperative governance in East Asia. The future efforts to build multilateral security cooperation system or CBMs should be comprehensive in its issue area and inclusive in its geographic range. Even though the multilateral cooperation system begins through bilateral efforts to build trusts and transparency, it should include more players around this region. The existence of neutral parties would precipitate the CBM process by mediating conflicting parties. The issues dealt with in the process should also be comprehensive, so that the negotiations can be facilitated by linking many different issues among the participating countries.

Key Words: OSCE, CBMs, East Asia, Multilateral Security Cooperation, Cooperative Governance

Introduction

Recently, the interest in cooperative governance in security areas is growing because the concept of security has extended in its content and range. In the past security meant traditional military security. However, current meaning of security is very comprehensive by including non-traditional threats such as economic crisis, human rights violations, terrors, environmental issues, maritime security, natural disaster etc. Then, these types of new security threats are very difficult issues to cope with unilaterally by any one country. Therefore, more and more scholars, government officials and states are paying attention to cooperative governance such as multilateral security cooperation to find solutions for these new security issues.[1]

Most recent discussions on cooperative governance is heating up in East Asia, especially in Northeast Asia because this region has faced various security challenges for several decades. In this area there are two nuclear weapons states—China and Russia—and is one country considered to have nuclear weapons—North Korea. The US is also a significant player in this region. There is antagonism between China and Japan, and Korea and Japan because of historical issues. Furthermore, the Korean Peninsula is divided into South and North. Between the two Koreas there are disputes over the Northern Limit Line on the West Sea.[2] These issues are not easy to resolve since most of them are related with more than two countries' interest directly and indirectly. Therefore, multilateral security cooperation system is rising as a plausible alternative mechanism to cope with these emerging security issues.

Since each region has unique history and culture, the prescription for each region should be based on tailored approach different from that of other regions. East Asia also has special historic and cultural tradition distinguished from other regions. However, it does not mean that we should not refer the cases of other regions. The cases of other regions would provide valuable lessons to develop cooperative governance system in East Asia. Among them, European case of multilateral security cooperation, especially the Organization for Security and Cooperation in Europe (OSCE) and its earlier version,

Conference on Security and Cooperation in Europe (CSCE) provides a role model of cooperative governance in East Asia. Europe established this cooperative governance system through confidence building measures (CBMs) embodied in the Helsinki Final Act of 1975. Even though the European system cannot be simply applied to East Asia, it is obvious that East Asian countries should make more efforts to build these CBMs and cooperative governance system in this region.

The second section will deal with the definitions and concepts of multilateral security cooperation. The next section introduces diverse facets of the European cooperative governance system, OSCE, Helsinki Final Act and CBMs. It will be followed by a section which discusses the possibility of multilateral security cooperation in East Asia. This article will be concluded by providing some directions to develop successful cooperative governance in East Asia.

What is Multilateral Security Cooperation?

Multilateral security cooperation goes beyond just a military alliance in which each member state is supposed to aid other member states attacked or perceived to be attacked by any common opponents. To cooperate under military alliances, member states prepare or declare war as an option to cope with common external threats. However, under multilateral security cooperation, member states make efforts to prevent or settle down the military conflicts among the countries. Multilateral security cooperation is special in that it pursues cooperation even among parties under conflicts, while military alliance is established between countries with perceived common threats.

Usually, multilateral security cooperation is performed through multilateral security regime, which is called as 'security community' among countries.[3] The 'community' is supposed to spread "mutual sympathy and loyalties; of 'we-feeling,' trust, and mutual consideration; [and] of partial identification in terms of self-images and interests."[4] Different from military alliances, a security community obligates states not to go for war against other member states. Furthermore, security community goes beyond merely preventing war and promotes a peaceful cooperation to resolve common socio-political issues. Rather than employing massive and violent military forces and power, security community institutionalizes interactive procedures to resolve conflicts among countries.[5] Therefore, the final goal of security community is to remove war or even the possibilities of war among states.[6]

There are two types of security communities according to the ways the communities are established. One is "amalgamated" communities where a common central government is structured by several previously independent political entities as we can see in the case of the US. In this case, the political entities concede the whole or part of sovereignty to the common central governments. The other type is "pluralistic" communities, which is composed of independent sovereign member states without forming common central governments.[7] Even though the member states in pluralistic security communities keep their own sovereignty, they "share the same identity, values and intentions."[8] These member states enjoy reciprocal interactions among each other.

According to Deutsch, there are two critical conditions which may promote the emergence of a security community. Most of all, participating states should be able to satisfy other members' needs and respond to their actions promptly in appropriate ways like communication or consultation through international organizations without resorting to violence. Forming security community through international organizations has merits in that those organizations can promote interactions between the member states and establish a common identity by finding common interests of the member states and forming norms of state behavior.[9] These contribute to preventing physical violence.

The other condition for emergence of security community would be if the political identities and orientations of the member states are compatible. Security community is supposed to have common values and similar identities. For example, even though geographic location of Australia and New Zealand are separated from European countries, they share the same identities and values with European countries. Thus, Australia and New Zealand are accepted as a part of Western security community.[10] In some way, even Japan is considered as a part of the Western security community because she shares the Western values. In this sense, geographical proximity of the states or ethnic origin of the peoples is not necessarily a precondition of security community.

However, building security community does not always need compatibility of values among member states. It is mutual needs and concessions which produce any agreements toward community of states even though those countries usually possess similar institutions, What leads to establishment of a security community is recognition by the states that military conflicts would not be attractive option to settle disputes among the political entities. As we can see nowadays, many security communities include states which do not share political identities and values. Rather, many successful security communities are composed of many conflicting countries.

The purpose of security community is to assure peaceful settlement of disputes among the member states without any physical conflict. The states which participate in security community "do not expect or prepare for the use of military force in their relations with each other."[11] Therefore, security community would be recognized as more useful and effective tool to keep peace among the countries under potential conflicts rather than the states with friendly relationships as we could see in the cases of Organization for Security and Cooperation in Europe (OSCE) and its earlier version, Conference on Security and Cooperation in Europe (CSCE).

This perspective considers security community as a space to build a common identity and practice cooperation among member states through bargaining and socialization. In this sense, international relationships can be expressed as "a world society of a political community, including social groups, the course of political communications, compulsory measures, and the submission to the most popular practices."[12] In fact, this concept of security community has spread to the area of military cooperation and hard politics. Cooperation in military affairs in Europe has begun from North Atlantic Treaty Organization (NATO), but later, it has extended to other countries in the Western Europe and then to the Eastern European states including Soviet Union. As the experience of cooperation has been accumulated among the countries, the realm of cooperation has extended from security affairs to economic and trade affairs. Nowadays, more and more non-traditional security cooperation has been brought within the mandate of security community. As a result, comprehensive security is emphasized by many scholars and decision-makers.

Multilateral Security Cooperation in Europe

The Helsinki Final Act, which was signed in 1975, faces the 40th anniversary in 2015. 35 heads of countries attended to sign the Act from Europe and North America. The 59 pages Final Act stated ten principles for further cooperation and a broader range of practical topics for the potential opponents and neutral states under the Cold War to cooperate each other. The 10 normative principles of the Act are very comprehensive and touches diverse issues and include "refraining from the threat or use of force, the inviolability of frontiers, peaceful settlement of disputes, non-intervention in the internal affairs of states, respect for human rights and fundamental freedoms and cooperation among states."[13] It was a small step to regulate the relations among the participating countries but a big progress to establish cooperative security regime.

The achievement in Helsinki not only strengthened European security for 40 years, but also the belief and spirit has spread to other parts of Europe. Beyond Europe, the Helsinki Act is regarded as a monument in commemoration of security cooperation even by other regions of the world. It has served as a paragon of collective security regime all over the world. However, the widespread benchmarking of the regime does not rest on its legal status. It was not a legal agreement. What provided the document authority were the intent and the spirit of the countries which signed the document. Even though the act was not legally binding, it has functioned as a political and ethical obligation to the related states. It is "principles along with a set of practical means of cooperation in three baskets—human, economic/environmental, and political-military securities."[14] The driving force of the Final Act comes from underlying political dedication undertaken by all the countries which have participated in the process.

It represented the start, rather than the end, of the process of defining cooperative security as a model for Europe. William Alberque summarized four other aspects of the Helsinki Final Act: [15]

> ➢ First, the Final Act opened a process that later developed in ways that never were anticipated. Looking back, that process had powerful and positive results. Its signatories thought that they knew what they had accomplished with the document, but the process has taken the Euro-Atlantic area on a journey few could have imagined in 1975.

> ➢ Second, the Final Act was tangible evidence of the change in German thinking about Europe. Germany played a central role in framing the issues and developing the ideas underpinning the Final Act. This demonstrated that a country previously seen as a threat to European security was now working to create a constructive and positive framework for collective action.

> ➢ Third, the Final Act did not seek to solve issues that were beyond resolution. For example, the neutral and balanced language related to boundaries proved to be extremely helpful during the seismic changes at the end of the Cold War, without addressing any of the specific boundary issues that existed during the late 1960s and early 1970s.

> ➢ Fourth, participating states were interested not only to stop the erosion in the security environment (though that was certainly one objective), but to find ways to make it better.

Confidence Building Measures (CBM) in the OSCE

The process establishing OSCE after Helsinki Final Act can be expressed as confidence building measures (CBMs). Confidence building measures are most important part of the long lasting conferences and dialogues in OSCE (CSCE). The fundamental purpose of the process was to reduce risks of armed conflicts by increasing transparency of the military maneuvers by each other. They believed that military conflicts among countries could happen just because any part of the blocs could not acquire enough information on the other side, and this lack of information could lead to miscalculation on the counterpart's intention and competence for military actions.

The confidence building measures raised "transparency, predictability, confidence and stability" by notifying military maneuvers in advance to each other and inviting observers to notifiable military activities in the region.[16] Especially, in the Conference on Disarmament in Europe held in 1986, the heads of the states agreed to expand the CBMs to confidence and security building measures (CSBMs) and imposed them as obligation to the member states. The success of the CSBMs in Europe stems from the fact that they were accomplished through broader and consistent efforts to boost dialogues and relieve the conflicts between the core countries in the Cold War.

The initial driving force of the CSCE process was Soviet Union's demands for dialogue to make the post World War II border permanent. The process was possible because the Western bloc responded to the demands. The Western bloc also had concerns about Soviet Union's military activities and capability. Furthermore, the Western bloc found the need for conference, as well, to expedite cooperation among European countries in diverse areas such as economic development, scientific technology and culture. This CBM process built up the conditions for stable disarmament which prevented chaos or armed conflicts during the collapse of Soviet Union as well as it promoted collapse of the Soviet regime.

Applicability of Confidence Building Measures in East Asia

The experience of CBM process in Europe provides valuable lessons for East Asia. Like Europe 50 years ago, East Asia is suffering from power conflict between two major blocs: US-Japan alliance vs. China. In East Asia where cooperation is critical for further economic development and political stability, the European experience for cooperation would become a very inspiring model. There are both optimistic and pessimistic predictions for East Asian multilateral security cooperation.

On one side, pessimistic perspectives argue that European model cannot be transplanted in East Asian regional context. They notice the diversity and complexity of East Asian political and cultural landscape around security issues. In Europe CBM process was possible because European countries shared relatively homogeneous political and cultural tradition in history. Before and after the HFA, Europe was clearly divided only into two blocs. It was apparent who allies were and who adversaries were. However, the two blocs shared pretty similar culture even though their political ideologies were divided. The division into two blocs was mainly due to the result of the World War II, not to historical cleavage.[17] On the contrary, in East Asia it is very hard to distinguish who the friends are and who opponents are even though there are two blocs competing. Even the US and China relationship is quite interdependent in economic development. The relationship between China and Japan is also very close. They need each other for further development. However, their political and military relations are competitive in nature. Furthermore, East Asian countries have not shared homogeneous political or cultural history except Chinese characters. This complexity of East Asian regional environment functions as a huddle against further cooperation in this region.

On the other side, a group of experts in East Asian regional politics contends that East Asia like Europe also has enough conditions to develop multilateral security cooperation system. There have been numerous meetings to find the relevance of OSCE experience in East Asia. Mautner-Markhof argues that there are certain similarities between the HFA and the "Basic Agreement between South and North Korea—officially known as the Agreement on Reconciliation, Non-Aggression and Exchanges and Cooperation between South and North Korea—that entered into force in February 1992."[18]

As such, each perspective toward the possibility of East Asian multilateral security cooperation system has its own reliable logic. While the pessimistic perspectives focus on the differences of political and cultural histories between Europe and East Asia, the optimistic perspectives emphasize the common demands for trust and transparency in both regions to build up stability, security and further development as the leading countries of world economy. However, the discrepancy between the two perspectives is not without a possibility of compromise. Europe in 70s and 80s and East Asia today has similarities in that they are core regions of international politics in each era. As the importance of the regional issues in the international politics increases, the pressure for building multilateral security cooperation and CBMs would expand as well.

Another factor we should not overlook among the factors which enabled HFA and CBMs in Europe was the existence of a group of neutral countries in the process. The neutral states precipitated the compromise by mediating the two confronting blocs. Since the neutral countries deeply engaged in the negotiation process, the European countries could make bold decisions with confidence. Without the neutral countries, the decisions would have been more difficult to achieve. These neutral countries include the European regional countries and out of region countries.

From the positive side multilateral cooperation in East Asia is needed because of economic interdependence in this region. The East Asian countries such as Korea, China and Japan assume more than 25% of the world GDP. The GDP share of the US and those three East Asian countries exceed a half of the total world GDP. Therefore, cooperation among those countries is very critical for further development of world economy. From the negative side the increase of transnational common threats volumes up the voices for multilateral security cooperation. As already discussed non-conventional threats including nuclear weapons, energy, environment, terrorism and natural disaster is increasing. These common threats do not discriminate and affect the countries in the region.

From the case of European CBM process, an important lesson could be learned. Security measures should be constructed as inclusive as possible. For substantive security building, it is necessary to include as many parties related to the regional security as possible in the process. Especially, the US and Russia should be included in the cooperative process to guarantee true security in the region. Even though those are not East Asian countries, in geopolitical terms, they are significant players in the region. In addition, to promote the negotiation process, it is also necessary expanding the range of the CBM process to the whole East and South Asia including major players in these regions like

India. As a neutral party, the countries like India could play a role to precipitate the negotiation by mediating the confronting blocs.

Conclusion

To build multilateral security cooperation in East Asia, it is necessary to set up elaborate roadmap for the process. Most of all, to overcome the diversities and complexities of the political and cultural history in this region, at the early stage, the confidence building process needs to simplify the relationships by reinforcing bilateral relations among Northeast Asian countries. Currently, the biggest hurdle for multilateral security cooperation in this region is complicated bilateral distrusts among the Northeast Asian countries: China-Japan, China-US, South Korea-Japan, South Korea-North Korea, North Korea-Japan, North Korea-US, Japan-Russia, US-Russia and so on. The types and areas of the disputes are also very diverse such as territorial, historical, nuclear, military and economic issues.

Then, the second stage should be focused on building multilateral cooperation system among Six Party Talks states as a platform for creating a security community. Bilateral relations are simplest to deal with, but it does not guarantee successful negotiations. Sometimes, the directions of mutual interests are not dyad but triangular or more complicated. Therefore, to solve those problem, all the countries directly involved need to sit on the same table. This multilateral talk would increase the possibility of success of negotiation through diverse deals.

Finally, it is desirable to extend the membership to Asia-Pacific regional countries beyond the Northeast Asia. Even though the Six Party Talks countries are core members of security issues in East Asia, talks among the counties directly involved is not enough for effective negotiations. Frequently, we notice the importance of mediators in international negotiations. Therefore, the participation of the third-party neutral countries would promote the success of the negotiations. In Asia, the ASEAN countries and India would be able to play the mediating role to the disputes in East Asia.

Endnotes

1   Hahnkyu Park, "Constructing 'positive' Regional Identity: A Challenge for Multilateral Security Cooperation in Northeast Asia," *Asia-Pacific Research*, Vol. 11, No. 1 (2004), p. 28-51.

2   See Samuel S. Kim, "North Korea and Northeast Asia in World Politics" in Samuel S. Kim and Tai Hwan Lee (eds.), *North Korea and Northeast Asia* (England: Rowman & Littlefield Publishers, Inc. 2002), pp. 3-58.

3   Karl W. Deutsch, *Security Communities, International Politics and Foreign Policy* (NY: New York Free Press, 1961), p 98.

4   Andrej Tusicisny, "Security Communities and Their Values: Taking Masses Seriously," *International Political Science Review*, Vol. 28, No. 4 (2007), p. 429.

5   Deutsch, *Security Communities, International Politics and Foreign Policy,* p. 98.

6   Tusicisny, "Security Communities and Their Values: Taking Masses Seriously," p. 426.

7   Ibid., p. 426.

8   Wang Jiangli, "Security Community in the context of non-traditional security," re-cited from Raymund Jose G. Quilop, "Building a Security Community in Northeast Asia: Options and Challenges," *International Journal of Korean Unification Studies*, Vol. 18, No. 2, (2009), p. 125.

9   Emanuel Adler and Michael Barnett, "Security Communities and Their Values: Taking Masses Seriously," *Security Communities as cited in Tusicisny*, p. 428.

10 Raymund Jose G. Quilop, "Building a Security Community in Northeast Asia: Options and Challenges," *International Journal of Korean Unification Studies*, Vol. 18, No. 2, (2009), p. 126.

11 Rosemary Foot, "Pacific Asia: The Development of Pacific Dialogue" in Lousie Fawcett and Andrew Hurrel (eds.), *Regionalism in World Politics* (New York: Oxford University Press, 1995), p. 233.

12 Amitav Acharya A., *Constructing a Security Community in Southeast Asia: ASEAN and the Problem of Regional Order* (London: Routledge, 2001)

13 Frances Mautner-Markhof, "Security Co-operation in Northeast Asia: The Relevance of Europe's Experience," *Global Asia*, Vol. 6, No. 4, (2011) p. 76.

14 William Alberque, "The Role of Political-Military Confidence and Security Building in the Northeast Asia Peace and Cooperation Initiative" presented paper in Northeast Asia Peach and Cooperation Initiative (Seoul: 2015), p. 1.

15 Ibid, p. 2.

16 Mautner-Markhof, "Security Co-operation in Northeast Asia: The Relevance of Europe's Experience," p. 77.

17 Alerque, "The Role of Political-Military Confidence and Security Building in the Northeast Asia Peace and Cooperation Initiative," p. 6.

18 Mautner-Markhof, "Security Co-operation in Northeast Asia: The Relevance of Europe's Experience," p. 77.

References

Acharya, Amitav A., *Constructing a Security Community in Southeast Asia: ASEAN and the Problem of Regional Order* (London: Routledge, 2001)

Acharya, Amitav. "Ideas, Identity, and Institution-Building: From the 'ASEAN WAY' to the 'Asia-Pacific Way'," *The Pacific Review*, Vol. 10, No. 3 (1997).

Adler, Emanuel and Michael Barnett (eds.), *Security Communities as cited in Tusicisny*, "Security Communities and Their Values: Taking Masses Seriously."

Alberque, William, "The Role of Political-Military Confidence and Security Building in the Northeast Asia Peace and Cooperation Initiative" presented paper in Northeast Asia Peach and Cooperation Initiative (Seoul: 2015).

Deutsch, Karl W., *Security Communities, International Politics and Foreign Policy* (NY: New York Free Press, 1961).

European Commission. 2001. "The European Union's Role in Promoting Human Rights and Democratisation in Third Countries", *COM* (2001) 252 final, 8th May 2001.

Foot, Rosemary, "Pacific Asia: The Development of Pacific Dialogue" in Lousie Fawcett and Andrew Hurrel (eds.), *Regionalism in World Politics* (New York: Oxford University Press, 1995).

Hammes, T., "War evolves into the fourth generation." *Contemporary Security Policy*, Vol.26, No.2, (2005).

Higgot, Richard, "Interregionalism and World Order: The Diverging EU and US Models." Telò, Mario (Ed.): *European Union and New Regionalism*, Aldershot, 2007.

Jachtenfuchs, Markus and Beate Kohler-Koch, "Governance and Institutional Development." In Antje Wiener and Thomas Diez eds., *European Integration Theory*, Oxford: Oxford University Press, 2004.

Keohane, Robert O., "Global Governance and Democratic Accountability." In David Held and Mathias Koenig-Archibugi eds., *Taming Globalization: Frontiers of Governance*, Cambridge: Polity Press, 2003.

Kim, Nam-Kook, "The Democratic Empire of the European Union: A Normative Leader or a Realist Compromiser?" *The Korean Journal of Defence Analysis*, Vol. 23, No. 4, 2010.

Kim, Samuel S., "North Korea and Northeast Asia in World Politics" in Samuel S. Kim and Tai Hwan Lee (eds.), *North Korea and Northeast Asia* (England: Rowman & Littlefield Publishers, Inc. 2002).

Manners, Ian, "Normative Power Europe. A Contradiction in Terms?" *Journal of Common Market Studies*, Vol. 40, No. 2, 2002.

Manners, Ian, *The Concept of Normative Power in World Politics*. Copenhagen: Danish Institute for International Studies, 2009.

Mautner-Markhof, Frances, "Security Co-operation in Northeast Asia: The Relevance of Europe's Experience," Global Asia Vol. 6, No. 4 (2011).

Park, Hahnkyu, "Constructing 'positive' Regional Identity: A Challenge for Multilateral Security Cooperation in Northeast Asia," *Asia-Pacific Research*, Vol. 11, No. 1.

Prodi, R., "2000-2005: Shaping the New Europe", *Speech to the European Parliament*, 15th February 2000.

Quilop, Raymund Jose G., "Building a Security Community in Northeast Asia: Options and Challenges," *International Journal of Korean Unification Studies*, Vol. 18, No. 2, (2009).

Smith, K., "The EU, human rights and relations with third countries: 'foreign policy' with an ethical dimension?" In Smith, K. and Light, M. eds., *Ethics and Foreign Policy*. Cambridge: Cambridge University Press, 2001.

Smith, K., 2008, p. 109; Grugel, Jean B., "New Regionalism and Modes of Governance - Comparing US and EU Strategies in Latin America." *European Journal of International Relations*. Vol.10, No. 4 (2004).

Tusicisny, Andrej, "Security Communities and Their Values: Taking Masses Seriously," *International Political Science Review*, Vol. 28, No. 4 (2007).

Chapter Four

Security Cooperation between Republics of India and Korea

Lalit Kapur

Barely a quarter of a century ago, anyone forecasting that India would have a role in East Asian security affairs or would be engaging with East Asian countries on security cooperation would have been treated with skepticism, even derision, by security analysts. India became inward looking after its wars in 1962, 1965 and 1971, first with China and then with Pakistan. Although non-aligned, American hostility (the beginnings of which have been attributed to the Korean War by Dennis Kux[1] and others) forced India to lean towards the Soviet Union, isolating itself from the network of alliances built up to contain that country by USA with much of East and Southeast Asia. The end of the Cold War saw India launching its Look East Policy in an attempt to reintegrate with the region. India's links with East Asia expanded towards the turn of the century, through development of trading relations with China, Hong Kong, Taiwan, South Korea and Japan. An important facet of trade is security, and the regional belief that India had a security role in East Asian affairs became evident from its being accepted as a member of the ASEAN Regional Forum in 1996[2] and a founding member of the East Asia Summit in 2005. Today, India has bilateral security dialogue or a declared strategic partnership with a number of East Asian countries, including the Republic of Korea (ROK), Japan, Vietnam, Singapore, Indonesia, China, Russia, Australia and USA.

The definition of security itself has changed substantially over the years. Security cooperation has both bilateral and multilateral components. This paper seeks to comprehensively explore bilateral security cooperation between the Republics of India and South Korea. It will do so under the following heads:-

(a) The changing concept of security.

(b) Indo-Korean security relations - a historical backdrop.

(c) Strategic imperatives and developments in bilateral security cooperation.

(d) Crystal gazing.

The Changing Concept of Security

The term 'Security Cooperation' conjures up images of military alliances designed to defeat a common enemy and preserve territorial security. These stem from the post-Westphalian construct, based on co-existing sovereign nation states and a norm of non-interference in each other's internal affairs. Subsequent European colonisation of a large part of the globe and domination of world affairs meant that the 'balance of power' aspect of security became central to the world order.

The retreat of colonisation and the economic rise of Asia have changed the very concept of security. Economic aspects have gained salience, with concerns about security of energy and resource availability and free movement of trade impinging directly on the concept of security. The emergence of non-state actors coupled with the increasing spread of terrorism, particularly in Asia; the challenge of combating pandemics; environment degradation leading to climate change; the spread of trans-national crime; and the myriad ways in which technology is changing the world all impact the concept of security today. Individual and human security concerns often come up against the needs of societal, state and regime security. In an increasingly interdependent world, security cooperation between nations, especially those as geographically separated as South Korea and India, needs to be viewed from the perspective of the multifarious needs of mutual security, rather than just security of territory.

Indo-Korean Security Relations – A Historical Backdrop

It is easy to forget India's millennia-old history of links with East Asia. Security linkages were visible when the Imperial Japanese Army attacked Hong Kong in December 1941, and the defenders included Indian troops from the Punjab and Rajput Regiments. Indian troops fought against the Japanese Army in Borneo, Singapore, Malaya and Burma before stopping them at Kohima, in Nagaland.

India played diplomatic and peacekeeping roles in Korea after World War II. An Indian, Mr KPS Menon, was Chairman of the UN Commission set up in 1947 to hold elections in Korea leading to the establishment of ROK. Following the September 1950 landings at Inchon, when American troops entered Pyongyang and approached the Yalu River, China conveyed warning of its impending intervention to USA through the Indian Ambassador at Beijing, Sardar KM Panikkar[3]. When this warning was ignored and 300,000 Chinese troops flooded into Korea, India sent the 60th Parachute Field Ambulance, a 627 member medical unit under Col Rangarajan, to tend to sick and wounded soldiers. The unit stayed in Korea from November 1950 to May 1954[4] and received a number of citations of merit from the Korean government, according to President Lee Myung-Bak[5]. When the armistice was signed in July 1953, India sent then Maj Gen KS Thimayya with a 6000 strong custodial force to chair the UN mandated Neutral Nations Repatriation Commission to oversee exchange of Prisoners of War by both sides. All these actions gave India a significant security role in the formative years of ROK.

However, ideological considerations during the Cold War saw India going in for insular and protectionist economic policies, isolating it from East Asia. Its end found India staring at a vastly changed geostrategic and geopolitical landscape. The emergence of Myanmar as a safe haven for insurgents belonging to India's North-Eastern states and their linkages with drug and arms smugglers in the Golden Triangle region of Myanmar, Laos, Cambodia and Thailand created a threat to national security, forcing India to seek cooperation from these Eastern neighbours. An unstable domestic environment characterised by Pakistan-aided insurgencies first in Punjab and then in J&K led to political instability, with short lived national governments that focused more on populist measures than building a stable economic system. To add to this, the first Gulf War of 1990-91 led to a hike in oil prices coupled with loss of income from remittances in Iraq and Kuwait, as well as from trade not only with these countries but also with erstwhile communist Eastern Europe, causing substantial loss of foreign exchange earnings and creating an economic crisis that forced India to seek an IMF bailout as well as to pawn its gold reserves. Collapse of the Soviet Union removed a major supporter on the international stage. India thus faced international isolation, collapsing economic security, loss of its prized strategic autonomy and the prospect of big power interference in its affairs. These factors forced the government to shift focus from ideological to economic concerns – and both ASEAN and East Asia were by this time emerging as economic success stories. The combination of these factors led to India re-engaging with the countries to its East, in the form of the Look East Policy (now the Act East Policy), which initially focused on ASEAN, but was expanded around the turn of the century to include Japan and South Korea.

Bilateral consular relations between India and ROK started in 1962 and were upgraded to the Ambassador level in 1973. Amongst the earliest examples of renewed 'defence' interaction (after the Korean War) was the visit of a 19 member team from India's National Defence College (NDC) to ROK in 1984[6]. The visit was repeated in 1986. The ROK NDU reciprocated by visiting India in 1987. In 1988, India's Oil and Natural Gas Commission placed an order for offshore patrol vessels on Korea Tacoma, now part of the Hanjin group. The first three ships of the class, Sukanya, Subhadra and Suvarna were built in Korea and delivered in 1989-90. Four others were subsequently built by Hindustan Shipyard Visakhapatnam under transfer of technology. The project led to an Indian Naval team being positioned at Masan, in Gyeongnam Province and the establishment of a Defence Wing in the ROK Embassy in New Delhi in 1990[7]. High level military visits commenced with the visit of India's Army Chief, General SF

Rodrigues, to ROK in 1992. The ROK naval training squadron visited Mumbai in October 1993. High level exchanges continued building up momentum and an Indian warship participated in the International Fleet Review at Busan in 1998, to mark the 50th anniversary of the Korean Armed Forces. The IN ship also participated in a joint exercise with ROK ships at this time.

Political and economic engagement had started improving when Prime Minister Narasimha Rao visited South Korea in September 1993 and President Kim Young-sam came to India in February 1996[8]. Following this, India permitted 100% FDI to Hyundai Motors and Samsung Electronics. Both would go on to become household names in India. In October 2004, President Rho Moo-hyun visited India and signed an agreement raising bilateral relations to a "Long Term Cooperative Partnership for Peace and Prosperity". A Memorandum of Understanding on cooperation in defence, industry and logistics was signed in 2005, while an MoU on cooperation between the two Coast Guards was signed in 2006. In January 2010, President Lee Myung-bak was the Chief Guest at India's Republic Day celebrations.

The years since have seen bilateral relations, including defence relations, picking up pace. A Memorandum of Understanding for cooperation in defence, industry and logistics signed between the two countries in 2005. This resulted in establishment of a Joint Committee, which has continued to meet regularly and identified numerous areas of cooperation. In January 2010, H.E. Mr Le Myung-bak visited India and was the Chief Guest at the Republic Day Parade. He and Prime Minister Manmohan Singh agreed to strengthen defence dialogue through regular high-level military exchanges as well as to explore joint venture cooperation in research and development and manufacture of military equipment, including through transfer of technology and co-production[9]. They also agreed to enhance bilateral relations to a Strategic Partnership[10]. In September 2010, the India Defence Minister Shri AK Antony became India's first Defence Minister to visit South Korea and signed two MoUs. The first, valid for a five year period, related to defence exchanges, including visits by ships, aircraft, training institutions and experts, as well as cooperation in humanitarian assistance and international peacekeeping. The second, between DRDO and ROK's Defence Acquisition and Procurement Agency, focussed on joint production and development of defence equipment. In June 2012, the first Trilateral Dialogue involving India, ROK and Japan (India's Institute of Defence Studies and Analysis, ROK's National Diplomatic Academy and Japan's Tokyo Foundation) was held. In November 2012, ROK's Minister for National Defence visited India. In June 2013, interaction at the level of National Security Adviser commenced with Mr Shiv Shankar Menon visiting Seoul. President Park Geun-hye visited India in 2014 and India's Defence Minister visited Seoul in April 2015. The Strategic Partnership between India and ROK was upgraded to a 'Special Strategic Partnership' during the visit of Prime Minister Modi to Korea in May 2015, making ROK only the second country with which India has a diplomatic and security dialogue in the 2+2 format, involving both defence and foreign ministers. An MoU on cooperation between the National Security Council Secretariat of India and South Korea's Office of National Security was signed.

Strategic Imperatives and Developments in Bilateral Security Cooperation

Notwithstanding the geographical distance separating them, the two nations have much in common. Both share the experience of being colonised, India by Great Britain and Korea by Japan. Both gained independence following World War II. Coincidentally, both celebrate the same day as their Liberation/Independence Day. Both North and South Korea gained independence from Japan on 15th August 1945 and their first governments were sworn in on 15th August 1948. India, on the other hand, obtained independence from Great Britain on 15th August 1947. The aftermath of independence saw both India and Korea being partitioned. India gave birth to Pakistan, while Korea was divided into North and South. Both India and ROK were subject to attack by China: ROK in October 1950, India in October 1962. India is Asia's third largest economy behind China and Japan, South Korea is the fourth. Both are democracies. Both are peninsular in character, necessitating a significant maritime outlook. Both are energy deficient and depend on secure SLOCs for import of their energy, which means both are dependent on freedom of the sea as well as unhampered and secure movement of trade for their economic growth. Both are concerned about rogue nuclear neighbours, though India views its concerns in this regard somewhat more seriously as the only target for Pakistan's nuclear weapons is India, whereas South Korea is not generally considered a target for North Korean nuclear weapons. However, both are concerned about the spread of WMD technology and the danger this poses to global and regional peace and security. Both are concerned about the terrorist activities of their estranged neighbour: the support Pakistan and more specifically the ISI provides to terror operations in India is now internationally recognised, while South Korea has its own experience by way of the Korean Air 858, ROKS Cheonan and incidents of firing such as on Yeonpyeong Island. Then there are complementarities, such as Korea's strength in electronics and hardware whereas India's lies in software, Korea's shipbuilding expertise vis-a-vis the slow rate of production in Indian shipyards, Korea's competitive defence technology vis-a-vis India's huge needs, estimated at over $ 100 billion in the next five years; and many more areas. These commonalities and complementarities ensure that the potential for bilateral defence cooperation is limited only by imagination.

Until the 1970's, South Korea's threat perceptions were shaped by fears of another North Korean invasion; terrorism sponsored by North Korea: a high military dependence on USA, including for manpower, intelligence and technology; and the involvement in Vietnam. President Park Chung-hee embarked on an ambitious military modernisation programme to increase the nation's indigenous weapons capability (this programme has now made South Korea an exporter of defence technology in recent years). The threat of war with North Korea declined in the 1980s and 1990s, but DPRK's formidable missile arsenal and withdrawal from the NPT in 2003 kept the threat alive. There was, moreover, the danger of regime collapse in North Korea, with consequential impact on ROK. The SLBM launch by DPRK on 09 May 2015 is only the latest of numerous overt threats to ROK.

Korea sits at the crossroads of continental and maritime Asia, in a region which has for long been the playground of great powers. Its history is of Russia, Japan, USA and China seeking to dominate its affairs, while Korea sought to retain its independence. The Korean War forced an alliance with USA and Japan which continues to this day. The Russian threat may have diminished, but a rising China remains a concern despite being ROK's largest trading partner and the source of much of its prosperity. Its export led growth has made it dependent upon international linkages, but it is yet to develop the capability to defend its interests wherever these exports go, or the source of its energy and raw material imports. Consequently, ROK needs to engage with global and regional powers, if only to ensure its economic security.

On the other hand, the Pacific face of Asia has become increasingly important to India's trade. China, Hong Kong, Indonesia, Japan, South Korea, Australia and Singapore have emerged as among India's largest trading partners[11]. The Pacific is vital for India's energy security: ONGC Videsh Limited has stakes in Russia's Sakhalin-I[12] and Imperial Energy fields, as well as Vietnam's Block 06.1[13]. Essar Oil has stakes in fields in Vietnam[14] and Indonesia, as well as a deal with ROSNEFT to import 10 million tonnes of crude per annum for the next 10 years[15]. GAIL is scheduled to import 2.5 million tonnes per annum of LPG from Russia for the next 20 years[16]. OVL and Oil India have MoUs to explore for hydrocarbons in the Arctic and East Siberia regions[17]. As India's appetite for energy grows, the search for oil and gas is bound to intensify - and the Russian Arctic has emerged as a new horizon for energy assets. Shipment of energy to India have to be through the Western Pacific and, as for China, energy security as well as security of energy flow have emerged as major concerns, impacting on the Indian economy as a whole.

Where trade goes, the flag will follow and security relations will develop. Already, Indian naval ships make annual forays into the Pacific, and this activity is bound to increase as trade and security needs grow. India needs partners in East Asia. From the Korean perspective, the immense Indian population offers a huge market that could significantly impact on Korea's GDP growth. It is recognition of these realities that have led to India and ROK becoming special strategic partners.

Security cooperation can be considered as comprising four broad heads: manpower, equipment, intelligence and leadership. The manpower aspect encompasses providing numbers to meet various security challenges, at the place they arise, their training and reach (ability to reach the area of interest). Equipment encompasses not only availability of the paraphernalia required by those combating security challenges (such as tanks, ships, aircraft, artillery, weapons, communication, electronics etc), but also its technological quality and maintainability. The third head, intelligence, relates to procurement and analysis of information relating to potential security challenges. The fourth, leadership, encompasses not only the desire to act together to assure mutual security, but also the creation of necessary structures as well as the strategy to tackle threats, both immediate and potential. In today's globalised world, a challenge may arise anywhere. Security cooperation is the ability of two or more countries to work together to address the challenge, using or supplementing each other's resources as required. It is an outcome of factors including a shared perception of the threat, a desire to commit manpower, equipment, money and other resources to deal with it and technological and industrial capability. The spectrum of potential areas of cooperation is vast, ranging from a full-fledged alliance at the top of the scale to development of military thought, intermittent cooperation in logistics, security of trade, training and intelligence exchanges at the lower end. In between are areas such as joint development and marketing of military equipment, cooperation in emerging technological domains including space, cyber and nuclear and many others.

A key area of cooperation has to be the spread of terrorism and the linked threat of WMD proliferation. Both India and ROK have been the victims of state sponsored terror, the former from Pakistan and the latter from DPRK. Collusion between Pakistan and DPRK is now well known. Neither India nor ROK have the ability to acquire intelligence, particularly relating to this collusion. It makes sense for the two to collaborate in this area. India's National Security Adviser, Mr Shiv Shankar Menon, in fact, broached the topic during his visit to Seoul in July 2013. The bilateral agreement on protection of classified military information signed by the two during President Park's visit to India in 2014 is a pointer towards incipient intelligence cooperation.

Another area is joint development of technology, as well as development and production of equipment. South Korea has emerged as one of the world's fastest growing exporters of defence equipment[18], although with a low base and sales limited so far to South East Asia. The country has successfully used an assertive offset policy to break into the highly competitive global arms export market, something from which India, which has been experimenting with offsets for many years, could learn. India is expected to spend $ 620 billion on 'defence' between 2014-2022, of which around 50 percent will be on capital acquisitions[19]. The market is currently dominated by USA, Russia, France, Ukraine and Israel, but other vendors have emerged, including from UK, Italy, Switzerland, Sweden and Germany[20]. With India having emerged as one of the biggest arms importers in the world, there is natural scope for Korean arms sales to India.

The successful sale of Offshore Patrol Vessels by Korea Tacoma to India has already been addressed. Subsequent attempts have not enjoyed similar success, though not for want of trying. Perhaps the most talked about example is Kangnam Corporation's abortive attempt to sell mine countermeasures vessels to India, after they won the global tender for supply of these vessels in October 2011. Two were to have been built in Korea and the balance six at Goa Shipyard (GSL) under a transfer of technology agreement. The losing bidder, Intermarine of Italy complained to India's Central Vigilance Commission as well as members of parliament about Kangnam Corporation having violated an integrity pact, which prohibited short-listed companies from using 'agents' to facilitate the deal[21]. The procurement process became stuck in red tape, the bid lapsed, and legal advice, which the government eventually accepted, was to cancel the acquisition process. Kangnam Corporation will have a chance to collaborate with GSL when proposals for construction of the MCMVs are invited again. The requirement has already been expanded to 12 ships[22] and the eventual requirement is likely to expand to 24.

Another abortive attempt was the offer of sale of 75 KT-1 basic trainer aircraft made by Korean Aerospace Industries (KAI) to the Indian Air Force in 2010. KT-1, the Beechcraft T-6C and Pilatus PC-7 cleared the technical evaluation at Jamnagar airbase, with the Pilatus PC-7 getting the contract in 2012. KAI protested about award of the contract to Pilatus on the grounds that their bid was incomplete and should have been disqualified; in fact the Korean Defence Minister wrote to his Indian counterpart requesting review of the decision[23]. As it stands, Pilatus will supply 38 more aircraft to the IAF, while the balance 68 required will, hopefully, be provided by the indigenous HAL[24]. The incident should be viewed in the same perspective as Airbus Industry's A330 beating Boeing's KC-46A Pegasus and IAI's 767[25] based design for a contract to supply four multi-role tanker transports to the ROK Armed Forces.

News reports in November 2015 indicate that ROK has successfully sold 100 of its locally designed and made Samsung TechwinK-9 155mm Self Propelled Howitzers to India for about $ 7.5 million each, beating a Russian 2S19 competitor to clinch the deal[26]. India's Larsen & Toubro will partner Samsung Techwin to manufacture this in India. The sale would appear to give ROK an edge in obtaining an even larger order for up to 400 towed 155mm howitzers, to be followed by manufacture of 1180 of them in India.

The examples above indicate that the ROK experience so far is a mixed bag. Any company hoping to do business in India, Korean or otherwise, will have to master the intricacies of India's much revised Defence Procurement Procedure (DPP). First brought out in 1992 as the master manual of capital defence procurement in India, it has been revised in 2002, 2003, 2005, 2006, 2008, 2011 and 2013, and is under review again as the Ministry of Defence tries to get its policy right. As of now, it categorises all defence acquisition decisions into four categories[27]: 'Buy', with two sub-categories based on whether the vendor is Indian or foreign; 'Buy and Make', which means purchase from a selected foreign vendor followed by licensed production/ indigenous manufacture in India; 'Buy and Make (Indian)', which means purchase from an Indian company forming a joint venture with the original manufacturer followed by licensed production/indigenous manufacture in India; and 'Make', which involves design, development and manufacture of high technology or complex systems or critical components and equipment entirely in India. DPP 2013 clearly identifies 'Buy Indian' as the most preferred category, followed by 'Buy and Make (Indian), 'Make', 'Buy and Make' and 'Buy (global)' as the last choice. The thrust is to make as much as possible in India; in fact during his visit to Korea in May this year, Prime Minister Modi invited South Korean companies to invest in the manufacture of defence equipment in India. This is an area with immense potential and Korean companies, with their rich experience of manufacturing for the Indian market, have sufficient experience in making joint ventures succeed, notwithstanding the odd hiccup.

Security technology offers another exciting area for cooperation. Numerous agreements have already been signed. One is on co-production and co-development of defence equipment between India's Defence Research and Development Organisation and Korea's Defence Acquisition and Procurement Agency. Intended to identify futuristic areas of interest for both in defence technology, the agreement envisages co-development and co-production, with marine systems, electronics and intelligent systems being priority areas. Another signed between the Indian Space Research Organisation and Korea Aerospace Research Institute in 2010 opens the doors for collaboration between the two in dual use areas, including in GPS where the Indian GAGAN (GPS Aided Geo-Augmented Navigation System) and KASS (Korea Augmentation Satellite System) and in Geographic Information Systems. Another agreement is on cyber security cooperation, to prepare against transnational cyber threats.

Yet another fruitful area for cooperation is in high level exchanges, designed to promote mutual understanding of each other's interests, concerns, methods, tactics etc. Both countries agreed to further enhance high level exchanges[28] during the visit of PM Modi to Korea earlier this year. They also agreed to strengthen partnerships between Indian and South Korean institutes of defence education, including NDC and KNDU, by sending officers to attend courses in each other's institutions; strengthening of National Security Council Structures of the two countries, commencement of staff level talks between the navies, regular exchange of visits between the two armed forces, cooperation in the area of UN Peacekeeping and an annual Track 1.5 dialogue.

Given the salience of the maritime domain for energy as well as SLOC security for both, maritime security should be among the focal areas of cooperation. The actual provision of security at sea will be a function of cooperation between the concerned maritime agencies of both countries. The agreement to commence staff talks at the Navy level will give a fillip to this cooperation, inevitably impacting on maritime security both in the Asia Pacific as well as in the Indian Ocean.

Some believe that India and ROK may share a common concern about a rising China. Both have a strong independent relationship with China, one that they will not sacrifice in a hurry. India established a "strategic and cooperative partnership for peace and prosperity with China during the visit of Premier Wen Jiabao in 2004[29]. China has emerged as India's biggest trading partner, with bilateral trade exceeding $ 70 billion last year. ROK re-established relations with China just over 23 years ago: till August 1992 China recognised only DPRK while ROK recognised only Taiwan. The 2007 free trade agreement has resulted in an explosion of bilateral trade. ROK exports to China in 2014 amounted to over $ 145 billion, 25.4% of ROK's total exports. In comparison, exports to USA were about $ 70.6 billion, while those to India were only $ 12.8 billion[30]. ROK also imported 16% of its total imports from China. More important, ROK has a trade surplus with China and will not easily antagonise its biggest trading partner. Its painstaking efforts to build linkages are evident from President Park Geun-hye's participation in the parade commemorating the 70th anniversary of the end of the Second World War in Asia.

There are three possible outcomes associated with China's rise. The first is that China remains a benign power and doesn't threaten anyone. This is an unlikely scenario, as both history and China's current posture in the South and East China Seas proves. The Chinese White Paper on Defence of May 2015 does not inspire confidence in this scenario, which in any case, is a best case which will not worry anyone. The second is that China becomes increasingly assertive, using military power to protect its interests, while USA continues to posture but does not take any significant action to moderate China's behaviour. This would open the region to Chinese hegemony, perhaps leading to all other nations uniting against China – but China has the ability to buy a lot of influence! The only effective counter to this eventuality would be of other powers combining to moderate Chinese behaviour– and the current climate seems to be of nations exploring such cooperation. The third option is that America opposes China's actions, leading to tensions and possible war. That would take the region into the forefront of a World War, as was sparked off twice in Europe by the rise of an autocratic Germany. The strategic environment thus seems to point to increased cooperation between regional nations, if only to balance China's rise and avoid a situation leading to either Chinese hegemony or another World War generated by the Thucydides trap.

Crystal Gazing

"Today's security environment is characterised by concerns over increased trans-national and non-military threats, including the proliferation of weapons of mass destruction (WMD), terrorism, piracy at sea and natural disasters. To make matters worse, security threats have become more complicated and multifarious involving disputes and conflicts pertaining to territories, resources, religions and races. Faced with this new security environment, countries around the world have endeavoured to maximise their national interests by strengthening their security capabilities at the comprehensive level and cooperating strategically with other nations while at the same time keeping them in check".[31] This quote from the South Korean Defence White Paper of 2010 is instructive. Though India doesn't have a defence white paper yet, the annual report by the Ministry of Defence talks of the same threats.[32] Given the congruity of views, bilateral security cooperation appears beneficial to both.

Looking to the future, perhaps the only spoiler in the bilateral security relationship are Seoul's continuing links with Islamabad and Delhi's with Pyongyang. So long as both sides are confident of each other's sincerity, these links will not mean much. It can confidently be predicted that India-ROK security relations will grow in the coming years. It can also be foreseen that the economic content of this relationship will comprise primarily of sales of Korean defence equipment to India, while geo-strategic concerns will focus on the maritime domain. An alliance against China is unlikely and will emerge only if forced by circumstances, but there is need for both nations to prepare even for the most unlikely of eventualities, building mutual confidence as well as interoperability.

Robert Kaplan had said, "The Greater Indian Ocean region, stretching Eastward from the Horn of Africa past the Arabian Peninsula, the Iranian Plateau and the Indian subcontinent, all the way to the Indonesian archipelago and beyond, may comprise a map as iconic to the new century as Europe was to the last one. Hopefully, the 21st century will not be as violent as the 20th...". Security cooperation between ROK and India plays a role in ensuring that peace and stability are maintained in the Eastern and Southern shores of Asia. It is for the leadership of both countries to ensure that bilateral cooperation grows, expanding into the multilateral arena where possible, to create a world safe for mankind.

Endnotes

1   President Truman is reported to have told a Congressman, "Nehru has sold us down the Hudson. His attitude has been responsible for our losing the war in Korea". See Dennis Kux, in "India and the United States: Estranged Democracies", published by National Defence University Press, Fort Leslie McNair, Washington DC, June 1993, P 74

2   See http://www.mea.gov.in/Portal/ForeignRelation/asean-regional-forum-august-2012.pdf, accessed on 21 August 2015

3   Dennis Kux, ibid, P 74

4   See http://indianexpress.com/article/sports/cricket/indias-cheer-group-in-pak-clash-korea-war-veterans/, accessed on 21 August 2015.

5   As quoted in http://timesofindia.indiatimes.com/india/Seoul-lauds-Indias-help-in-1950/articleshow/6072928.cms, accessed on 21 August 2015.

6   Skand Tayal in 'India and the Republic of Korea: Engaged Democracies', published Routledge in cooperation with ICWA, 2014, ISBN 978-1-138-02036-8, P126-127.

7   Ibid, P 127

8   Dates of all visits from Embassy of India, Seoul website, see http://www.indembassy.or.kr/pages.php?id=22 accessed 01 August 2015.

9   "India-Republic of Korea Joint Statement: Towards a Strategic Partnership". Sourced from http://www.idsa.in/resources/documents/India-KoreaJointStatement.25.1.html on 02 August 2015.

10 Ibid

11 Based on data collated from Directorate General of Commercial Intelligence and Statistics, Ministry of Commerce and Industry, sourced from http://www.dgciskol.nic.in/data_information.asp on 12 December 2015.

12 Utpal Bhaskar, in "Halliburton, Baker Hughes Pull Out of OVL's Russian Oil, Gas Field", published in Live Mint, 07 April 2015, see http://www.livemint.com/Industry/ljLLIh5OOB7PgWe4WcUcsN/Halliburton-Baker-Hughes-pull-out-of-OVLs-Russian-oil-gas.html

13 PTI, published in Live Mint, 27 August 2015, see http://www.livemint.com/Industry/xrwj3JAZ37CFZ2n5QTohMK/ONGC-gets-oneyear-extension-for-Vietnam-block.html

14 See http://www.essar.com/article.aspx?cont_id=yjQVyWGHXKQ=, accessed on 12 December 2015

15 PR Sanjai and Promit Mukerjee, in "Essar Group, Rosneft Explore Part-Crude, Part-Cash Deal", published in Live Mint, 21 July 2015, see http://www.livemint.com/Companies/dDPWZxbHefAVhWxQBMiDuJ/Essar-Group-Rosneft-explore-partcrude-partcash-deal.html

16 Daniel fineren in Reuters report, "GZAPROM, India's GAIL Agree 20-yr LNG Sales Deal", see http://www.reuters.com/article/russia-india-lng-idUSL6E8L1DXG20121001

17 PTI report "OVL Inks Deal with Russia's ROSNEFT to explore hydrocarbons", published in Indian Express, 25 May 2014, see http://indianexpress.com/article/business/companies/ovl-inks-deal-with-russias-rosneft-to-explore-hydrocarbons/

18 See http://www.ft.com/cms/s/0/66a9a33a-42ea-11e3-8350-00144feabdc0.html, accessed 20 Aug 15.

19 Rajat Pandit, in "India's defence imports 40 times its export basket", Times of India, 29 November 2014, see http://timesofindia.indiatimes.com/india/Indias-defence-imports-40-times-its-export-basket/articleshow/45313520.cms

20 Ibid

21 See http://timesofindia.indiatimes.com/india/Deal-for-S-Korean-minesweepers-to-be-scrapped/articleshow/45171910.cms, accessed on 20 August 2015

22 See http://www.thehindu.com/news/national/air-force-to-get-38-more-pilatus-basic-trainers/article6948865.ece, accessed 20 Aug 15

23 See http://ajaishukla.blogspot.in/2015/02/defence-ministry-official-questions.html, accessed on 20 Aug 15

24 See http://www.thehindu.com/news/national/air-force-to-get-38-more-pilatus-basic-trainers/article6948865.ece, accessed 20 Aug 15.

25 James Drew in "Airbus Beats Boeing in South Korean Tanker Competition", published in Flight Global, 30 June 2015, see https://www.flightglobal.com/news/articles/airbus-beats-boeing-in-south-korean-tanker-competition-414161/

26 Indian Defence News, 09 November 2015, sourced from http://www.indiandefencenews.in/2015/11/indian-artillery-deal-south-korea-does.html on 10 November 2015

27 DPP 2013 may be accessed from http://mod.nic.in/writereaddata/DPP2013.pdf

28 India ROK Joint Statement for Special Strategic Partnership (18 May 2005), sourced from http://www.mea.gov.in/bilateral-documents.htm?dtl/25261/India__Republic_of_Korea_Joint_Statement_for_Special_Strategic_Partnership_May_18_2015

29 See http://in.chineseembassy.org/eng/ssygd/zygx/t191496.htm, sourced 10 December 2015

30 See http://www.worldstopexports.com/south-koreas-top-import-partners/2285, accessed 20 Aug 15

31 Opening paragraph of introduction to 'Section I: Global Security Landscape' in South Korea's 2010 Defence White Paper.

32 See articles 1.6, 1.7 and 1.30 of MoD Annual Report 2014-15, http://mod.nic.in/writereaddata/AR1415.pdf

Chapter Five

Nuclear Security Issues: Challenges and Opportunities
(North Korea's Nuclear Threat Perspective)

Yong Soo Kwon

Korea National Defence University

Introduction

Despite its weak economy and the international sanctions, threat of North Korea's nuclear weapons and missiles have been significantly increased since the mid-2000s. The country's growing threats clearly pose a security challenge not only for Northeast Asia, but also for the international community. Pyongyang already operates various missiles with a range of up to 3,000 to 4,000 km, and much of the related technology is mature. It is widely estimated that North Korea has already taken initial steps towards fielding a nuclear-tipped intercontinental ballistic missile (ICBM) KN-08, although it remains untested. In the year 2014, North Korea carried out more than 100 flight tests of tactical ballistic missiles including projectiles. It also conducted two successful submerged ejection tests of SLBM in May and December 2015, respectively. North Korea could be as little as a year away from deploying a submarine armed with a nuclear-tipped missile.[1]

In addition, the nuclear threat has also become a serious challenge to the international community as well as South Korea. Practically, nuclear weapon program of North Korea began in 1980s. In the mid of 1980s, North Korea reached a dangerous level of nuclear capacity with advancements due to increased Soviet support for the nuclear program.[2] The North also had begun a Highly Enriched Uranium (HEU) program in the 1990s through cooperation of the nuclear technology with Pakistan. It is believed that North Korea has been assembling actual HEU capabilities since 2000. In February 2005, Pyongyang announced its possession of nuclear weapons. It has subsequently carried out four nuclear tests since 2006. Even after the third test in 2013, Pyongyang has continued to threaten the world with another nuclear test and showed its signs. On 6 January 2016, North Korea announced that it conducted a successful test of a miniaturized hydrogen bomb. It is, however, estimated to be a partial hydrogen bomb test.[3]

A technical assessment is, therefore, essential to understand the North Korean nuclear threat, and to create a basis upon which an appropriate response to the future advancements can be formulated. From this perspective, this article provides a technical analysis of North Korea's nuclear weapon capability. Beginning with a brief history of this program development, I analyse Pyongyang's nuclear capability in terms of core issues, such as explosive yield of nuclear tests, miniaturization of nuclear weapons, HEU program, number of the weapons, and North Korean ICBM KN-08 as a delivery system. Finally, it presents challenges of North Korea's nuclear threat from the assessments made by the article.

Threat & Proliferation of Ballistic Missile

Over thirty-nine countries have operated ballistic missiles as an asymmetric strategy. In particular, North Korea's growing nuclear and missile capabilities pose a security challenge not only for Northeast Asia, but also for the international community. Its ICBM development is becoming a reality. The ballistic missile's threat may be explained from three perspectives as follows: firstly, it could be delivery means of Weapons of Mass Destruction (WMD) like nuclear biological and chemical warheads; secondly, it flies at supersonic speeds over atmosphere during the most of the flight time. It is, therefore, hard to intercept the missile in the midcourse phase; finally, It is difficult to estimate the exact trajectory during the re-entry phase due to tumble, or corkscrew movement.

North Korea has been one of the world's most active suppliers of ballistic missile systems since the mid-1980s. More than 40 per cent of the world trade of the ballistic missile supplied to the developing world was from North Korea in 1987-2009.[4] In addition, more than 80 per cent of the North Korea's total units in 1987-93 were delivered to the Middle East.

The History of Nuclear Weapon Developments

1. Missile Development[5]

North Korea first entered the missile business in the early 1960s. Between the late 1960s and the early 1970s, North Korea acquired many other types of missiles from Moscow and China. This included the capability for full-rate production of the HY-2 (Silkworm) system. By the early 1980s, Pyongyang was also producing most of its components, with the exception of a sustainment motor and guidance components. Around the same time, North Korea received two Scud-B missiles from Egypt, which it reverse-engineered, and reproduced domestically for export. This was a turning point for Pyongyang's indigenous missile industry. Production of North Korea's domestic production lines for these new Scuds began to gradually yield fruit from 1985. The Scud-C was first tested in June 1990, and entered full-scale production by 1991. Eager to earn revenue and political benefits from clients abroad, North Korea began to actively export these full systems to countries in the developing world, including Iran, Syria, and Pakistan.

Over time, the North Korean missile complex grew more capable of extending the range of its arsenal. The Nodong missile – which is capable of reaching Japan – was successfully tested in May 1994. The missile with a range of up to 1,300 km was the first to feature important modifications from the Scud design. Yet it was only in the 1990s that Pyongyang sought to develop missiles that could be classed as 'long-range'. The first multi-stage rocket with a range of 2,500 km, the Taepodong-1, was launched in a space configuration in August

1998. Around the same time, Pyongyang also began to develop the Musudan system, which is capable of striking the US military base in Guam. This missile was first operationally deployed in 2007 and boasted a range of 3,000-4,000 km.

In the mid-1990s, North Korea began to develop the three-stage Taepodong-2: the first stage involved the clustering of four Nodong missiles, while the second stage used a single Nodong engine. Though it represented a technological advancement, tests of this system continued to show the North Korean missile research and development complex's struggles. When this missile was first tested in 2006, it flew for about forty seconds before exploding. A modified version of this space-launch vehicle, capable of putting Alaska in its crosshairs, was attempted again in April 2009.[6] However, it was not until December 2012, that the broader expert community became attentive to the fact that North Korea might be overcoming previous substantial difficulties in its long-range missile programmes. As mentioned above, it launched its Unha-3 (the space-launch variant of the Taepodong-3) and successfully put a satellite into orbit. This system is capable of delivering a warhead up to 10,000 km, and the success of the test is difficult to ignore.

The North Korea's provocative actions by projectile and short ballistic missile tests have become more serious. In the year 2014, North Korea carried more than 100 flight tests. It even conducted three submerged ejection tests of SLBM in 2015. Pyongyang's official Korean Central News Agency (KCNA) said that the test on 9 May was a successful underwater test launch of a strategic ballistic missile from a submarine.[7] Some Western analysts contended that the missile was ejected from a submerged barge. It is, however, obviously done to test the submerged ejection of the missile. In addition, North Korea carried out a successful ejection from a submerged submarine on 21 December 2015, but despite these developments, it remains years away from having an operational system.

North Korea revealed a modified version of KN-08 ICBM in its 10 October 2015 parade celebrating the 70th anniversary of the Workers' Party of Korea. The missile was first seen at North Korea's military parade in April 2012. The configuration shows that it is getting better and closer to the real ICBM model than its previous ones. It is widely estimated that North Korea has already taken initial steps towards fielding the nuclear-tipped KN-08.

2. Nuclear Weapon Development

While North Korea's nuclear research commenced in the mid-1950s, its program only became concrete only decades later. In the years between 1950s and 1970s, North Korea's nuclear program was primarily focused on basic training and research. In the 1950s, North Korea tried to acquire basic knowledge to initiate its nuclear program and began to send its scientists and engineers to the Soviet Union for training. In the year 1959, North Korea concluded a nuclear cooperation agreement with the USSR.

However, the practical nuclear weapon program began only in 1980s. North Korea had built a factory at Yongbyon to refine yellowcake and produce fuel for reactors from 1980 to 1985.[8] At the same time, North Korea began to operate facilities for uranium fabrication and conversion,[9] and conducted high explosive detonation tests to further its weapons development. In the mid of 1980s, North Korea reached a dangerous levels of nuclear capacity with advancements due to increased Soviet support for the nuclear program. In 1985, they joined the Nuclear Non-proliferation Treaty (NPT). Despite the 'Agreed Framework' between the United States and North Korea in October 1994, North Korea had continued the nuclear weapon program. It was reported that the North Korea began a Highly Enriched Uranium (HEU) program through cooperation of the nuclear technology with Pakistan. In 1990s, A. Q. Khan (who was the father of Pakistan's nuclear program) visited North Korea at least 12 times.[10] Pakistan provided uranium-enrichment information to North Korea in exchange for missile technologies.

In the year 2002, the U.S. intelligence community had become convinced that North Korea was pursuing a HEU capability in violation of the Agreed Framework. It estimated that the North Korea had been assembling actual HEU capabilities since 2000 and that it had been 'seeking centrifuge related materials in large quantities' since 2001.[11]

In 2003, North Korea announced its withdrawal from the NPT and reactivated its one functioning nuclear power plant. In February 2005, Pyongyang had announced its possession of nuclear weapons. This is Pyongyang's most definitive public claim to date on the status of its nuclear arsenal.[12] In addition, after expelling IAEA inspectors in April 2009, North Korea claimed for the first time that it was proceeding with its own uranium enrichment program. North Korea carried out four nuclear tests since 2006. The two first nuclear tests in 2006 and 2009, are estimated to have been of plutonium based nuclear devices. The third one was conducted in February 2013, amidst speculation that it may have been of a new uranium-based design, or of a 'miniaturised' device.

After the third test in 2013, Pyongyang has continued to threaten the world with another nuclear test and showed its signs. On 6 January 2016, North Korea announced that it conducted a successful test of a miniaturized hydrogen bomb. The test was widely reported on social media shortly after it took place based on detection of a 5.1 magnitude seismic event. Meanwhile, South Korean authority officially announced that it registered magnitude 4.9 and yielded only a 6 kilotons explosion. Based on the low yield, many analysts remained sceptical of its claim and expressed the possibility of a boosted fission device test. Lee Sang-cheol, the top non-proliferation official at the South Korean Defence Ministry, told a forum in December 2015 that although Mr. Kim's hydrogen bomb boasts might be propaganda for his domestic audience, there was a 'high likelihood' that North Korea might have been developing such a boosted fission weapon.[13] It is worthwhile to note that it might be a partial hydrogen bomb. According to Bill Gertz's article,[14] preliminary U.S. intelligence estimates have concluded that North Korea's fourth underground nuclear test involved a small explosion that could be a component of a larger-scale thermonuclear device.

Assessment of North Korea's Nuclear Capability

North Korea's nuclear and missile capabilities are generally regarded as advancing, but along a path that contains notable technological obstacles to functioning of the capabilities. An assessment of the country's current capabilities shows that uncertainty still exists about whether North Korea has managed to overcome some of the hurdles that analysts believe are in their way.

Explosive Yield of Nuclear Tests

It is hard to say exactly the magnitude of the nuclear explosive yield. The explosive yield could be different depending on the site's geology and what kinds of measures are used to calculate. The measures can be inferred in remote sensing ways and scaling law calculations based on blast size, infrasound, fireball brightness, seismographic data, and shock wave strength.

North Korea has conducted four nuclear tests since 2006. The first test yield was less than one kiloton, and the second test was a large yield of two to six kilotons. South Korean Defence Ministry said that its third test in 2013 calculated by the seismic waves indicated a blast of six to nine kilotons[15] though competing assumptions about the site's geology leave some doubt over the accuracy of this assessment. According to the special event report of Incorporated Research Institutions for Seismology (IRIS), the yield of the North Korea's test in 2013 is estimated at 19.8 kilotons, with minimum and maximum yields of 14.8 and 39.5 kilotons.[16] While the Federal Institute for Geosciences and Natural Resources (BGR), a state-run geology research institute in Germany, places the estimate to be 40 kilotons.[17] If the explosive yield were six to nine kilotons, as reported by the South Korean authorities, this would suggest that North Korea still lacks the ability to miniaturize its warhead and would need additional nuclear tests to achieve it.

On 6 January 2016, North Korea claimed that it conducted a successful test of a miniaturized hydrogen bomb. South Korean authority officially announced that it registered magnitude 4.9 and yielded only a six kilotons explosion, although some institutes said that the fourth test was detected up to a 5.1 magnitude seismic event. It is important to note that the seismic event magnitude and estimated yield are significantly different depending on the institutes and scaling law calculations as seen in table

Table 1. Estimated Explosive Yield

Nuclear Test	seismic event magnitude (Institute)	Estimated Explosive Yield			
		KMA (Korea)	CTBTO (IMS)	Murphy (U.S.)	KKI
6 January 2016	4.8 (KMA)	6kt	6.3kt	12.6kt	16kt
	4.9 (CENC)	-	7.9kt	16.2kt	22kt
	5.1 (EMSC, USUG, IRIS)	-	12.6kt	29.8kt	45kt

Miniaturization of Nuclear Weapons

It is believed that North Korea may be more capable in warhead miniaturization than yield-based analyses would imply. Bruce Klingner said that North Korea has possibly, already achieved warhead miniaturization, the ability to place nuclear weapons on its medium-range missiles, and a preliminary ability to reach the continental US with a missile.[18] A. Q. Khan claimed, for example, that during a visit to North Korea in 1999, he was shown boxes containing components of three finished nuclear warheads, which he was told could be assembled for use atop missiles within an hour.[19] He also stated that North Korea's nuclear weapons were the perfect nuclear weapons, technologically more advanced than Pakistan's own.[20] It is important to note that these suggestions were made even before the first North Korean nuclear test in 2006.

Admittedly, Khan's testimony does not shed light on which types of missiles he felt the warheads were suitably miniaturised for. It is generally estimated that North Korea can fashion warheads of sizes appropriate for delivery aboard short- and medium range systems such as the Nodong. A North Korean statement in 2002 suggested that its scientists had assembled between two and five nuclear warheads and that some of those were likely fitted to the Nodong missiles.[21] Given the decades since North Korea first fielded the Nodong missile, and given North Korea's history with the now-defunct A. Q. Khan network in Pakistan (which would have been able to nuclearize this system), the assertion that the Nodong is nuclear-capable is reasonable.

There is another important fact about North Korea's nuclear weapon miniaturization. According to 'North Korea's Nuclear Weapons: The Great Miniaturization Debate', held by 38 North on 5 February 2015, North Korea already seems to reach a significant level of technology to miniaturize nuclear weapons through three nuclear tests. It seems very plausible that North Korea have a nuclear weapons design somewhere in the Mark 12 to Mark 7 range of 450 to 750 kg in mass with a diameter between 60-90 cm.[22] Some experts have pointed out that North Korea could probably do much better, trying out something like the Mark 12 which weighted on 450 kg. In the early of 1980s, Chinese provided a uranium-based design to Pakistan that was 500 kg and 90 cm in diameter, which the Pakistanis miniaturized and passed on to Libya.[23]

Highly Enriched Uranium (HEU) program

A second area of uncertainty surrounding the North Korean nuclear program pertains to the country's ability to weaponize uranium. Pyongyang's nuclear program was originally plutonium-based, as evidenced by the nuclear infrastructure in the country prior to its first weapons test. Yet it is clear that North Korea also feels it necessary to simultaneously pursue a uranium enrichment campaign, opening a second path to a bomb. It has invested significant resources into constructing facilities that would be able to produce weapons-usable highly enriched uranium, some of which are - clandestine. In November 2010, North Korea disclosed a uranium nuclear facility with 2,000 centrifuges similar to the Pakistani P2 to visiting U.S. scientist Siegfried S. Hecker and the quantum of the centrifuge is being referenced to assess HEU nuclear weapon capabilities. However, the -centrifuge numbers are likely to be even more high. For example, A. Q. Khan who knows North Korea's nuclear network well assessed that NK had 3,000 or more centrifuges by 2002. Olli Heinonen, former the Director-General for Safeguards, Director at IAEA, estimated that NK was likely developing a 5,000 centrifuge enrichment capability. According to his study,[24] Pyongyang was successful in procuring large quantities of high strength aluminum from Russia and the United Kingdom in 2002-03. A simple tally of the amounts and types of equipment and material sought by North Korea suggests that it planned to develop, at least, an A. Q. Khan HEU production scheme, which requires about 5,900 centrifuges. That means a 5,000 centrifuge strong enrichment capacity.

After Prime Minister Benazir Bhutto's state visit to North Korea in 1990, it was reported that the highly sensitive information was being exported to North Korea in exchange for missile technologies.[25] In the year 1993, classified information on uranium enrichment was delivered to North Korea in exchange for information on developing ballistic missiles.

While South Korea's Defence Ministry has not officially stated that Pyongyang can produce weapons-usable HEU, in his November 2013 statement to the National Congress, the Minister did acknowledge that North Korea could manufacture nuclear weapons using this material.[26] Despite official South Korean silence on the matter, the international community generally accepts that North Korea has tried to produce HEU,[27] particularly given the tour of uranium facilities at Yongbyon that it offered to visiting expert Siegfried Hecker in 2010.

This would be worrying news. Compared to plutonium-based designs, HEU-based models are more easily miniaturised, reducing the need for underground testing. The process of manufacturing HEU is also more difficult for external eyes to detect and monitor, adding greater uncertainty to analyses of the status of the nuclear programme. However, at this stage it would be prudent to assume that if North Korea has not yet produced and weaponised HEU already, it will attain the ability to do so in the coming years.

Number of Nuclear Weapons

According to CNN news on 24 April, Chinese military expert said North Korea may have double the number of nuclear weapons than previously believed.[28] It means North Korea may have twenty warheads not ten as previous US forecasts held. Stockpile of weapons could grow to fifty or even one hundred within next five years.

Nuclear weapon number depends on the amount of weapons grade reprocessing plutonium and design skill. It is believed that North Korea has acquired amount of 40 kg the plutonium through three to four spent fuel reprocessing.[29] It is capable to produce nuclear weapons of six to ten warheads. But, some experts estimate that NK could produce more than ten. That number might be estimated under the assumption that the North Korea's technology is at medium level as seen in Table 2. It significantly depends on the nuclear technology maturity level

Table 2. Number of Nuclear Weapon

Explosive Yield	6kt		10kt		20kt	
Technical Capacity	Low	Medium	Low	Medium	Low	Medium
Weapon Grade Plutonium (kg)	4	2.5	5	3	6	3.5
Number of Nuclear Weapon	10	16	8	13	6	11

Source: Yong Soo Kwon, "North Korea's Nuclear Threat", Northeast Asia Seminar, 19 October 2015.

In addition, North Korea's HEU nuclear capability is also as serious as the plutonium program. As mentioned above, the international community generally accepts that North Korea has tried to produce HEU, particularly given the tour of uranium facilities at Yongbyon that it offered to visiting expert Siegfried Hecker in 2010. Physicists estimate that it North Korea may be capable of producing 20 to 80 HEU annually, or approximately one to four bombs' worth. If one assumes that North Korea has been producing HEU at this rate since November 2010, and that 20kg is sufficient for one warhead produced along the lines of A. Q. Khan's designs, Pyongyang may have been able to produce between four and seventeen nuclear weapons by the end of 2015.

North Korean ICBM, KN-08

North Korea's road-mobile ICBMs are also clearly in the works, but had not yet been tested or operationally deployed. It is also widely estimated that North Korea has already taken initial steps towards fielding a nuclear-tipped ICBM. Mock-ups of the KN-08 were first seen at North Korea's 15 April 2012 military parade. In his testimonial to the a Senate panel on 12 March 2013, National Intelligence Director James Clapper testified that, "we believe North Korea has already taken initial steps towards fielding this system, although it remains untested".[30] North American Aerospace Defence (NORAD) Command head Adm. William Gortney also told reporters during a Pentagon briefing, "our assessment is that they have the ability to put a nuclear weapon on a KN-08 and shoot it at the homeland", and "that's the way we think, that's our assessment of the process".[31]

On 10 October 2015, North Korea revealed a modified version of KN-08 ICBM at a parade celebrating the 70th anniversary of the Workers' Party of Korea. Compared with the old versions shown in 2012 and 2013, the important differences are as follows: two stage design instead of three stages, larger first stage, different second stage, different warhead and/or post boost system, reduced total length.[32] The whole design looks much more mature than the old version, and the overall quality of the mock-ups is much better.[33]

Regarding the looming operationalization of the system, Frank Jannuzi, a former Senate staffer known for his expertise on North Korean issues, said: "they're closer now than they were six months ago and they'll be closer six months from now than they are today."[34] The opinion of this author is that we are likely to see the operational deployment of the KN-08 in the next few years.

Table 3. Old and New KN-08 Design

Design Characteristics	Old	New
Stages	3	2
Stage Diameters	~ 2 m, ~2 m, ~ 1.3 m	~ 2 m, ~2 m
Total Length	~ 19 m	~ 17 m
Cable Duct/Raceway	only at tanks	from base to top
Stage Separation Rockets	chaotic locations	sensible locations
Visible Warhead Length	long	short
Front Shape	conical warhead	blunt
Mock-up Quality	very poor (2012) poor (2013)	average (2015)

Source: Markus Schiller and Robert H. Schmucker, 'Getting Better-The New KN-08 Design', ST Analytics (28 October 2015), p. 3.

Challenges of North Korea' Nuclear Threat

In terms of its nuclear program, North Korea will require to successfully 'miniaturise' its warheads to fit atop a missile such as KN-08 and/or an SLBM. In simplistic terms, the lighter the warhead, the longer the potential range of the missile, hence the need for so-called 'miniaturization' of its nuclear bombs. North Korea asserts that it has already conquered this problem. Its state-run news agency claimed in 2013 that a 'miniaturized nuclear device with greater explosive yield' had been successfully tested underground. North Korea also announced that it conducted a successful test of a miniaturized hydrogen bomb on 6 January 2016. Although many analysts have remained sceptical of its claim, North Korea seems to reach a significant level of technology to miniaturize nuclear weapons through four nuclear tests. As Jeffrey Lewis mentioned above, it seems very plausible that North Korea have a nuclear weapons design somewhere in range of 450-750 kg mass with a diameter of 60-90 cm.

As delivery systems of a nuclear weapon, road mobile KN-08 ICBM and North Korean SLBM (Bukkeukseong-1) may be good options. A modified version of KN-08 was revealed during a parade in Pyongyang on 10 October 2015. It is getting better than the old versions shown at 2012 and 2013 military parades. The whole design looks much more mature than the old versions, and the overall quality of the mock-ups is much better. It is widely estimated that North Korea has already taken initial steps towards fielding the missile, although a full flight test remains to verify the re-entry vehicle technology. If some technical problems including reliability, nuclear warhead miniaturization and re-entry vehicle technology are solved, its capability to strike the continental United States would be assured. From a technical perspective, it seems possible that North Korea will overcome the remaining obstacles which it faces over the course of the next few years. North Korea conducted at least ten rocket engine tests for KN-08 including one test in July 2015 and completed construction to upgrade its Sehae long-range rocket launch site. It is believed as a final step before the KN-08 flight test, but it is more likely to deploy initial operations without the flight test like the Musdan missile. However, decision to test or operationally deploy missile systems seem to be politically- and strategically-driven decisions rather than technically driven. Nevertheless, it is safe to assume that North Korea's achievements of nuclear weapon and nuclear-tipped missile capabilities including SLBM are a question of 'when' not 'if'.

If North Korea deploys submarines with nuclear-tipped SLBMs, it may be a game changer. North Korea also successfully conducted two underwater ejection tests of a SLBM in 2015, though test in late November failed. North Korea has been continuing to actively pursue its SLBM development program and modernize the Sinpo South Shipyard since the submerged ejection test in May 2015. However, there is a higher likelihood of conducting partial development tests to improve the missile reliability and accelerate the SLBM deployment. Thus, it is important to establish a phased adaptive strategy because there is a high possibility that the missile flight test may be a strategic decision.

Endnotes

1   J.S. Chang, 'N. Korea successfully conducts SLBM test last month: U.S. report', *Yonhap New Agency,* 5 January 2016.

2   Jacques E. C. Hymans, 'Assessing North Korean Intentions and Capacities: A New Approach', *Journal of East Asian Studies* (Vol. 8, Issue 2, May 2008), pp. 259-292.

3   Bill Gertz, 'North Korea Tested Partial Thermonuclear Device' *The Washington Free Beacon,* 7 January 2016.

4   Joshua Pollack, 'The Evolution of North Korea's Ballistic Missile Market', *Nonproliferation Review* (Vol. 18, No. 2, July 2011).

5   Yong-Soo Kwon, 'An assessment of North Korea's Nuclear and Long Range Missile Capabilities', *Uncertain Trajectory: Implications a Long-Range North Korean Nuclear Capability* (Seoul: RINSA-RUSI, 2014), pp. 7-8.

6   FAS, 'North Korea's Taepodong and Unha Missiles', <http://www.fas.org/ programs/ssp/nukes/nuclearweapons/Taepodong. html>, accessed on 7 January 2014.

7   Kelsey Davenport, 'North Korea Tests Missile for Submarine', *Arms Control Today,* 2 June 2015.

8   *American Security Project,* 'North Korea's Nuclear Program', Update 12 March 12 2013, <http://www.Americansecurityproject. org/north-koreas-nuclear-program/> accessed 20 November 2015 .

9   C. P. Vick, 'KN-08: Hwasong-13 the Semi-mobile Limited Range ICBM', Update 18 November 2015, <http://www.globalsecurity. org/wmd/world/dprk/kn-08.htm>, accessed 20 November 2015. Some sources claim the facility becomes operational in 1986, while others claim 1990(Joseph S. Bermudez, 'North Korea's Nuclear Infrastructure,' *Jane's Intelligence Review* (February 1994), p.75.

10 NTI, 'North Korea Nuclear Chronology', Revised February 2011, <http://www.nti. org/media/pdfs/north_korea_nuclear.pdf?= 1316543714>, accessed 20 November 2015.

11 Morton I. Abramowitz, James T. Laney and Eric Heginbotham, *Meeting the North Korean Nuclear Challenge* (Council on Foreign Relations, Independent Task Force, 2003), <http://www.cfr.org/content/publications/ attachments/Korea_TF.pdf>, accessed 3 October 2015.

12 Arms Control Association, 'Chronology of U.S.-North Korean Nuclear and Missile', Updated: May 2015, <https://www.arms control.org/factsheets/dprkchron>, accessed 3 October 2015.

13 David E. Sanger and Choe Sang-Hunjan, 'North Korea Says It Has Detonated Its First Hydrogen Bomb, *The New York Times,* 5 January 2016.

14 Bill Gertz, *op. cit.*

15 South Korea's defence ministry said the event reading indicated a blast of 6–7 kilotons, later revised to 6–9 kilotons using the Comprehensive Nuclear Test Ban Treaty Organization's calculation method. (Choi He-suk, 'Estimates differ on size of N.K. blast', *The Korea Herald,* 14 February 2013).

16 *IRIS,* 'Special Event: North Korea nuclear explosion', Updated 5 November 2015, <http://ds.iris.edu/ds/nodes/dmc/ specialevents/2013/02/12/north-korea-nuclear-explosion/>, accessed 1 August 2015.

17 Christian Bönnemann, 'Nordkorea: BGR registriert vermutlichen Kernwaffentest', Hannover, 12 February 2013, <http:// www.bgr.bund.de/DE/Gemeinsames/ Oeffentlichkeitsarbeit/Pressemitteilungen/BGR/bgr-130212_Kernwaffentest-Nordkorea.html>, accessed 1 August 2015.

18 Bruce Klingner, 'Allies Should Confront Imminent North Korean Nuclear Threat', 3 June, 2014, <http://www.heritage.org/ research/reports/2014/06/allies-should-confront-imminent-north-korean-nuclear-threat>, accessed 24 August 2014.

19 R. Jeffrey Smith and Joby Warrick,'Pakistani Scientist Depicts More Advanced Nuclear Program in North Korea', *The Washington Post,* 28 December 28 2009.

20 David Albright, "North Korean Miniaturization," 13 February, 2013, <http://38north.org/2013/02/albright021313/>, accessed 17 August 2014.

21 *Missile Threats,* 'Nodong-1', <http://missilethreat.com/missiles/no-dong-1/>, accessed 2 September 2014.

22 Jeffrey Lewis, 'North Korea's Nuclear Weapons: The Great Miniaturization Debate', 05 February 2015, <http://38north.org /2015/02/jlewis020515/>, accessed 29 August 2015.

23 *Ibid.*

24 Olli Heinonen 'Nuclear Proliferation Concerns – The North Korea Case', 2 November 2012, <http://live.belfercenter.org/files/ Olli%20Heinonen_Nuclear %20Proliferation%20Concerns_The%20North%20Korea%20Case.pdf>, accessed 24 August 2014.

25 *Revolvy,* 'Abdul Qadeer Khan'. <http://www.revolvy.com/main/index.php?s= Abdul%20Qadeer%20Khan>, accessed 20 July 2014.

26   <http://news.chosun.com/site/data/html_dir/2013/11/21/2013112100354.html>, accessed 12 December 2013.

27   Mary Beth Nikitin, 'North Korea's Nuclear Weapons: Technical Issues', CRS Report for Congress, 3 April, 2013.

28   Tim Macfarlan,' Korea may have DOUBLE the number of nuclear weapons previously believed, say Chinese military experts', *Daily MailOnline*, 24 April 2015.

29   IAEA concluded that North Korea has probably reprocessed spent fuel on three to four occasions since 1989 (FAS, 'Yongbyon - North Korean Special Weapons Facilities', <http://fas.org/nuke/guide/dprk/facility/yongbyon.htm>, accessed 12 December 2015).

30   Rachel Oswald, 'North Korea Won't Have Operational Mobile ICBM Without Testing: Engineer,' *NTI Global Security Newswire*, 22 March 2013.

31   Aaron Mehta, 'US: N. Korean Nuclear ICBM Achievable', *Defencenews*, 8 April 2015.

32   Markus Schiller and Robert H. Schmucker, 'Getting Better-The New KN-08 Design', ST Analytics (28 October 2015), p. 2.

33   *Ibid.*, p. 3.

34   Jae-soon Chang, '(LEAD) N. Korea conducts new engine test for KN-08 ICBM: think tank', *Yonhap NEWS*, 2 October 2014.

Chapter Six

Nuclear Security Issues: Challenges and Opportunities

Dr Roshan Khanijo

Global Nuclear Environment

Nuclear Security during the Cold War era was confined to issues like weapons proliferation, theft and accidents. However, in a changing global environment, this definition has expanded and become more holistic in nature. Aside from the areas mentioned above, 'Nuclear Security' must now also include "the prevention, detection, and response to, criminal or intentional unauthorized acts involving or directed at nuclear material, other radioactive material, associated facilities, or associated activities[1]". Therefore; there has been a shift in the threat perceptions of 'Global Nuclear Security' and these facets need to be taken into consideration in order to keep up with the evolving nuclear security architecture.

The rapid increase in energy demand and the limited availability of clean, renewable sources of energy supply has led to a shift towards nuclear energy and the consequent emergence of 'Civilian Nuclear Power Plants' world over. The safety and security of these budding power plants and the threat potential that the fissile material possess, is something that needs to be factored into any Global Nuclear Security framework. If adequate measures regarding the safeguarding of the same are not taken soon, then the power plants remain at the risk of becoming potential targets for terrorist groups, making the threat of 'Nuclear Terrorism' not merely a terrifying possibility but a probable reality. "The threat level has been further enhanced by the presence of the state-non-state dyads, and the sharply adverse relationships between states and non-state actors, such as terrorist groups, that are potentially capable of acquiring and utilising nuclear or radiological weapons"[2]. Globally, there are over 435 commercial nuclear power reactors, operable in 31 countries, capable of generating 375,000 MWe of electricity, and another 70 more reactors are under construction[3]. In Asia alone, one finds that there are 123 operable nuclear power reactors, another 41 are under construction, and there are plans to build additional 92 power plants[4]. Asia, in particular, is thus witnessing a surge in the construction of nuclear power plants, especially in West Asia (UAE, Iran, Turkey, and Saudi Arabia) and South East Asia (Vietnam, Thailand, and Philippines) where nuclear reactors are being planned. Pakistan also has two mega nuclear power plants under construction while two are still being planned. Also, the growing military nuclear stockpiles of Pakistan, is a cause of concern. Thus the security environment in Asia is precarious and volatile, especially the Afghanistan-Pakistan region. Furthermore, China's economic prosperity has provided it with the means and the motivation to reinforce its military strength. It has engaged in a systematic modernization spree via the development of niche technologies in the nuclear and space domains, adding volatility to the geostrategic security framework. The current nuclear security challenges in Asia, therefore, emerge from the twin threats of rapidly expanding civil nuclear power plants and its vulnerabilities due to lack of universal nuclear safety and security norms; and the upsurge of nuclear weapons, leading to an enhanced threat perception in this region. Therefore both these issues lead to an increase in the nuclear instability, and they also actively increase the proliferation risk, making the region vulnerable to nuclear terrorism.

Three Tier Global Nuclear System

The current global nuclear environment is a 'Three Tier Nuclear System'. The first tier consists of the P5 nations and the declared NWS, like India, Pakistan, North Korea and Israel. While Israel has not openly declared its nuclear status, researchers are certain about

Israel's nuclear weapon capabilities and intentions. The second tier includes 'Threshold Nuclear States' such as Japan, South Korea, Iran and Taiwan, who may not have nuclear weapons at present but possess the requisite technology and expertise for the development of these weapons in the future. The only exception to this tier is the case of Iran, which has theoretically signed the 'Nuclear Deal', which should serve as a block if not a ban on the development of nuclear weapons. But the fact of the matter remains that signing the deal cannot necessarily be considered the equivalent of following the deal to its logical conclusion. Furthermore, several researchers believe that Iran already has the basic technology required to develop nuclear weapons, and that its continuous efforts to improve its missile program makes it a potent adversary to the stability and security in West Asia.

The third tier of 'Aspiring Nuclear Weapon States' was created by the President Dwight D. Eisenhower's "Atom for Peace" program. The Americans, initially provided aid for the construction of nuclear reactors in several nations such as Iran, Israel and Pakistan, under the garb of the "Atom for Peace" program. Since then the civilian program has spread rapidly and several countries are beginning to adopt this technology. While most of these nations are bound by the Nuclear Non-Proliferation Treaty (NPT), the dual nature of this technology remains a potent risk, because despite the best intentions, this accessibility of fissile material provides nations with the option to redirect the fuel and technology for furthering military purposes. Additionally, the non-binding nature of the NPT provides nations with an escape hatch that allows them to leave the treaty on the basis of flimsy loopholes, as was demonstrated by North Korea and Iran

Despite these concerns, measures are being taken to raise and ensure nuclear safety and security around the world. The International Atomic Energy Agency (IAEA), is trying to make countries aware of the imminent threats that affect nuclear power plants through their various safety and security initiatives. Additionally, through its 'Additional Protocol' mechanism, the NPT has also been trying to control nuclear proliferation. However, all these mechanisms are voluntary, non-binding, and non-punishable, which makes it easy for nations to ignore or violate them. The other issue at stake is, 'Global Nuclear Disarmament', which has remained a distant dream. Further,

Russia's revival of nuclear strategy and the American refusal to abandon its ballistic missile technology as well as its development of global prompt precession missile systems, acts as a motivator for China to develop its missile and space technologies. All these changes are having a cascading effect on Asia. It has led to an imbalance in the Asian power structure as Chinese military modernization serves as a threat to the stability in the region. Furthermore, this has led to several power plays and geostrategic alliances within the region such as the nuclear collaboration between China and Pakistan which has led to the latter developing Tactical Nuclear Weapons (TNWs) and consequently lowering the nuclear threshold in Asia. Pakistan and China's nuclear programs, both pose major causes of concern for Asia, albeit for different reasons. Pakistan is attempting to escalate tension by lowering the nuclear threshold whereas China is qualitatively and quantitatively increasing, diversifying and modernizing its nuclear weaponry in order to keep up with the changing global security paradigms. Another country in Asia that is also creating tremendous amounts of instability is North Korea, however, that aspect is being dealt by my colleague, and hence, this paper will focus on nuclear issues concerning China and Pakistan.

Modernization Trends and the Upsurge in Nuclear weapons

a) Pakistan Fissile Material: Production Trends

Nuclear stability in Asia is increasingly becoming a major cause for concern and it has remained one of the central agenda points for security issues and debates worldwide. The country which remains the focal point of this discourse and adds to the geostrategic vulnerability in the region is indubitably Pakistan. Nowhere is there a greater nexus between nuclear proliferation and terrorism as there is in Pakistan. While on one hand Pakistan has the world's fastest growing nuclear arsenal, on the other hand the largest concentration of groups bent on acts of terrorism[5] resides in the Afghanistan-Pakistan region. Furthermore, Pakistan as a nation raises questions about the very security of the state and thus the security of its nuclear crown jewel[6] due to its growing fundamentalism, ethnic violence, weak political institutions, and fragile economy. For the last few years, Pakistan has been bent on steadily enhancing its capabilities to produce nuclear fissile material. In 1998, China helped Pakistan in constructing a Heavy Water Moderated reactor at Khushab (which has produced 6-12 kg of Plutonium per year since it was operationalised). With the passing of time several more reactors have also been added to Khushab. Additionally Pakistan also has a Uranium Enrichment plant at Kahuta, and has constructed three Plutonium production units at Khushab, while the fourth one which is under construction, will soon be completed. There have been several expositions and theorizations of Pakistan's fissile material capabilities. In the beginning of 2013, Pakistan had a stockpile of 100-200 kg of Plutonium which was sufficient to make about 16-40 weapons[7]. The International Panel on Fissile Materials stated in 2013 that Pakistan possesses fissile material sufficient to build over 200 weapons. As far as Highly Enriched Uranium (HEU) is concerned Islamabad has a stockpile of approximately 3.1 tons of HEU and produces enough HEU for perhaps 10 to 15 warheads per year[8]. These estimates might have been higher if Pakistan had used advanced centrifuges (P3/P4 Model). Furthermore, according to the global fissile report of 2015, the total HEU for military use in Pakistan is 3.1 Metric Tons and separated Plutonium is .17 Metric Tons[9]. However, there is a clear disparity in terms of the number of nuclear weapons which Pakistan possesses. Washington based nuclear specialists Hans Kristensen and Robert Norris have estimated, that in 2010, Pakistan had 160-249 warheads, and since then, the number has grown substantially, while on the other hand Stockholm International Peace Research Institute (SIPRI) 2015, chose to put forth a more conservative view and has estimated this number at around 100-120. However, it is believed that Pakistan can increase its bomb output by 60 per cent above typical estimates, if it uses a composite core combining a 2-3 kg plutonium sphere surrounded by HEU shell[10].

b) Pakistan's Modernization and Weaponisation Trends

Pakistan's nuclear policy is based on the concept of 'First Use' of nuclear weapons and they profess that they will not hesitate in using the same even under attack by conventional weapons. Especially so, if their four redlines are violated. This is why they have consistently rejected the relatively more stable policy of 'No First Use'. The four thresholds/

redlines for Pakistan's engagement with nuclear retaliation are the transgressing of their space threshold, military threshold, economic threshold and domestic destabilization; all of which were instituted in order to dissuade India from attacking them.

Pakistan's main objective has always been to develop a strategy of 'Full Spectrum Response'; which is why they developed the TNWs. With the development of 'Nasr' they can now propagate the case of 'Early Use' of nuclear weapons, if they ever felt that the Indian columns entered their territory. While they've developed the miniaturized TNW, 'Nasr' (which has a range up to 60 km and assumed to carry a sub kiloton nuclear war head) for skirmishes on the lower end of the spectrum, they've also developed their MRBM Shaheen, along with other gravity weapons for retaliation on the higher end. This, TNW trajectory is a dangerous and incredibly volatile progression as there remain doubts regarding the security of the agencies that 'Command and Control' these highly dangerous weapons. This is linked to core concerns regarding the operationalization of TNWs, which would need to be deployed in the battle field and where responsibility for them lies completely with the local commanders. This easy accessibility towards such dangerous volatile material increases the security risks associated with nuclear weapons and makes them more vulnerable to theft, accidents and risk of unauthorized launch. These threats will in turn lower the nuclear threshold in Asia and make the region even more vulnerable to nuclear terrorism. Pakistan has already witnessed a terrorist attack on their naval dockyard in September 2014, when their Pakistani Naval Dockyard in Karachi was attacked by terrorists from the sea. Armed with grenades, assault rifles, and rocket-propelled grenades, the terrorists could have inflicted considerable damage to highly secure naval assets if they had the opportunity[11]. This particular attempt was foiled by the 'Ready Reaction Force', but if the terrorist attempt had been successful, the consequences would have been catastrophic. Therefore questions about safety and security standards become doubly important, considering the fact that offshore facilities are difficult to protect from attacks from the sea by non-state actors. Additionally Karachi is also a highly volatile area due to the presence of a large number of terrorist groups such as Tehreek-e-Taliban (TTP),

Badar Mansoor, Punjabi Taliban, Al Mukhtar Group, Kharooj, Al Furqanetc[12] which makes it even more vulnerable to external and internal threats.

Pakistan has made significant progress in modernizing its nuclear arsenal and increasing importance is being given to Plutonium weapons over Uranium. This is also one of the major reasons why Pakistan is trying to enhance Plutonium production. They have also redoubled their efforts towards developing TNWs which require the miniaturization of warheads. Plutonium serves as a more effectively pliable base material and would therefore be preferred over the Uranium. Furthermore they are also attempting to make nuclear tipped cruise missiles with conventional diesel-electric submarines aimed at developing a sea-based variant of its nuclear-capable, indigenously produced Babur missile (Pakistan navy conducted cruise missile tests from naval platforms in 2012[13]).This is part of their strategy aimed at ensuring 'Sea Based Deterrence' which will only intensify the volatility and threat perceptions in the geostrategic region.

c) China's Modernisation Trends

Within the Asian subcontinent, China is also modernising its nuclear forces by developing a new generation of mobile missiles, with warheads consisting of MIRVs and penetration aids[14]. Its potent triad consists of Land-Based Platforms which include the DF-31A and has successfully tested advanced DF 41 with MIRV capabilities. Its Sea-based Platforms include JIN-class SSBN and eventually this will carry CSS-NX-14 (JL-2) SLBM with an estimated range of 7,400 km and together these will give the PLA Navy its first credible long-range sea-based nuclear capability[15]. "It is believed that China has a total of 250 nuclear warheads. China has a substantial fissile material stockpile consisting of some 16 Metric Tons of HEU and 1.8 Metric Tons of weapon grade Plutonium; so there are no practical constrains on its ability to produce an arsenal of any size it chooses. Given the choices China makes in regard of its delivery systems, it could deploy anywhere up to an additional 150 warheads"[16]. Further, with such an arsenal, China also has the capability for escalation dominance vis-à-vis weaker nuclear adversaries[17], which will force other nations to reassess their deterrence capabilities and further heighten the geostrategic tension.

As far as development of niche technology is concerned, China has been wary of US intentions for a while. Therefore, its main aim has been to attempt to decrease the strategic gap between the two countries. The speed with which China is trying to develop its technological capabilities (especially in the area of space and information) is a cause of concern for other countries in Asia, and China's testing of hypersonic glide vehicles in 2014 is a testimony to this change. These threat perceptions are thus pushing countries towards reviewing and redefining their internal security structures.

Nuclear Proliferation

The spread of nuclear weapons and the proliferation of nuclear technology and information, to a non-NWS has always been a major cause for concern. However; there have been historical instances of countries choosing to work against the interests of a global nuclear zero and selectively imparting nuclear knowledge, and material to the non-nuclear states. Pakistan and North Korea are examples of this process. These nations could only develop nuclear weapons because their mentors provided them with the requisite technology to do so. While it is widely believed that the NPT has been able to contain and control the issue of nuclear proliferation to a large extent, the fact of the matter is that the treaty has been violated umpteen times both by aspiring as well as P5 nations. The latter have in fact been more central to the conflict and there have been instances where they have been seen either assisting rogue states or ignoring the proliferation issues altogether, solely for the purpose of increasing their national spheres of influence. US's inadequate measures to control Israel and Pakistan's nuclear program and China's assistance to Pakistan and North Korea, are just two examples of how the problem of proliferation has a problematic if not downright appalling lineage in the past.

These problems, have further multiplied in the second nuclear age where Pakistan and North Korea, have become major proliferators of nuclear technology. There has been research and documentation of the Pakistani scientist Mr. AQ Khan and his network in acquiring and proliferating nuclear technology to states like Iran, North Korea and Libya. This network, which had its tentacles in over 20 countries and sold Pakistani nuclear technology for at least 16 years, was finally exposed in 2003 by the interdiction of German-registered ship, with its cargo of Uranium enrichment equipment bound for Libya's nuclear weapon programme[18].The major unspoken and unaddressed cause for concern remains the fact that the activities of Mr. Khan might have happened in conjunction with the Pakistani authorities. The reason for this speculation arises from Husain Haqqani's, (former adviser to Nawaz Sharif) statement that "The Military had...always been in charge of Khan-in that all of its activities were governed by their orders[19]". Eventually under military pressure, even Mr. AQ Khan confessed to the same story but it was clear that this was a subterfuge being strung in order to placate the Americans. This is further evinced by the fact that a blind eye was turned to these nefarious activities and Mr. Khan also received a subsequent pardon from the then President Pervez Musharraf. Yet when he attempted to open the skeleton box once again, he was placed under immediate house arrest and prevented from exposing the networks of power orchestrated by the scientist and the army.

Another country that might covertly benefit from Pakistan's help is Saudi Arabia. Pakistan has a close ideological and strategic relationship with Saudi Arabia as the latter has provided economic help and bailed out Pakistan on several occasions. Also Western researchers allege that Saudi Arabia had also invested heavily in Pakistan's defence sector, especially its missile and nuclear labs[20]. Prior to the Iran Nuclear Deal, Gary Samore, who was President Barack Obama's counter-proliferation adviser until March 2013, stated in Newsnight that "I do think that the Saudis believe that they have some understanding with Pakistan that, in extremis, they would have claim to acquire nuclear weapons from Pakistan[21]." This statement, while inflammatory is a very real possibility since Saudi Arabia already has the delivery vehicles for the missiles. In fact, in the late 1980s they had bought dozens of CSS-2 ballistic missiles secretly from China. Apart from this, the nuclear cooperation and kinship demonstrated by Pakistan and North Korea repeatedly cannot be ignored. AQ Khan has made documents available that prove that he personally transferred more than $3 million in payments by North Korea to senior officers in the Pakistani military, who subsequently approved his sharing of technical know-how and equipment with North Korean scientists[22].

North Korea also has a disconcerting history of proliferating nuclear technology. North Korea is alleged to have proliferated ballistic missile technology to the Middle East, especially to Iran. Further, North Korea has a track record of selling advanced military technology like ballistic missiles to numerous pariah nations[23]. Recent research also suggests that North Korea is looking towards Saudi Arabia now for support, as the latter has the requisite financial resources to support them in their drive for military modernization. Such an arrangement is potentially mutually beneficial for both countries. It will provide Saudi Arabia with an alternative in case Pakistan backtracks and refuses to oblige them with technology or information and Saudi Arabia could provide North Korea with financial support in exchange. However it must be stated that while theoretically such a quid pro quo situation seems mutually beneficial, the countries involved in this trilateral power nexus happen to be extremely volatile, to say the least. The various indices dictating these transactions could lead to an imbalance that would affect not only the regional but the global security framework as well. Nuclear proliferation, therefore; becomes a huge risk, especially when it stems from those nuclear weapon countries that are internally unstable and have weak economies. The complete lack of an effective democratic institution makes the tyrannical ruler/military the sole arbiter of the decision making process and the complete unaccountability that the leader is provided with makes these nations a risk to global peace.

Nuclear Terrorism

In legal terms, according to the 2005 United Nations International Convention for the Suppression of Acts of Nuclear Terrorism[24] nuclear terrorism is an offense committed if a person unlawfully and intentionally "uses in any way radioactive material ... with the intent to cause death or serious bodily injury; or with the intent to cause substantial damage to property or to the environment; or with the intent to compel a natural or legal person, an international organization or a State to do or refrain from doing an act." Nuclear terrorism can be triggered either by acquiring a nuclear weapon through theft/purchase via the black-market; using a crude explosive device built by terrorists or by nuclear scientists,(who the terrorist organization has furtively recruited); and lastly by using an explosive device constructed by terrorists and their accomplices using their own fissile material or the acquisition of fissile material from a nation-state.[25]

Aside from the above mentioned guidelines, issues that also need to be taken into consideration are cyber threats and 'Dirty Bombs' or Radiological Dispersal Device (RDD). The RDD is a combination of radioactive material fused with conventional explosives in an attempt to create a more dangerous and volatile conventional weapon. While not as dangerous as whole scale nuclear attacks, dirty bombs are the more plausible and imminent threat, as radioactive devices are the easiest to make due to easy accessibility of radiological materials which are widely used in the civilian sector (For example X-RAY, food processing etc). Additionally, there has also been a substantial dispersal of nuclear fissile material due to rapidly burgeoning civilian nuclear sector worldwide. Currently, global fissile material (namely Uranium) is about 13450 Tons, of which 99 percent is with NWS, while the Plutonium stockpile is estimated at 500 tons and half of this is in the civilian sector[26]. Due to the complete lack of any standardized safety and security mechanisms, this fissile material may become a potential target for theft. Those countries whose civilian plants do not fall under IAEA supervision are at greater risk to nuclear terrorism. The IAEA Illicit Nuclear Trafficking Database notes 1,266 incidents reported by 99 countries over the last 12 years, including 18 incidents involving HEU or Plutonium trafficking.[27] There have been 18 incidents of theft or loss of HEU and Plutonium confirmed by the IAEA.[28] The non-state actors driven by ideology and state support both in terms of finance and the space provided by the state can have the means to succeed in their plan, however irrational that may seem. In Asia, the country which is the epicenter of terrorism is Pakistan. As seen in the past, Pakistan has not only the history of nuclear proliferation, but its scientist was also involved in the nuclear black market which has been discussed previously. Almost all major terror groups have direct or indirect affiliation to Pakistan. The Al Qaida leader, Osama bin Laden had contemplated of using nuclear device. The Islamic State jihadist group (ISIL) had stated that it could obtain a nuclear weapon within 12 months, according to the latest issue of the ISIL's propaganda magazine Dabiq.[29]An article attributed to British photojournalist John Cantlie held hostage by the ISIS for over two years[30], states that "The Islamic State has billions of dollars in the bank, so they call on their wilayah in Pakistan to purchase a nuclear device through weapons dealers with links to corrupt officials in the region". Various independent studies carried out by strategic think tanks found that "Pakistan .... Nuclear stockpile faces immense threats, both from insiders who may be corrupt or sympathetic to terrorists and from large-scale attacks by outsiders[31]". The reason can be because "the region has more violent extremists than any other area making the country unstable, and its arsenal of nuclear weapons is also expanding[32]". Thus nuclear terrorism is no longer a dystopian alternative future but probably a very disturbing reality that needs to be addressed.

The Way Ahead- Nuclear Security Cooperative Mechanism

Bilateral cooperation between the US and the erstwhile USSR played a critical role during the Cold War era in ensuring nuclear stability. However, with the change in the geostrategic global power nexus, the emergence of asymmetric warfare and the increased dispersal of nuclear technology, the global environment requires new security paradigms in order to maintain a secure and stable nuclear architecture. While the possibility of a global 'Nuclear Zero' has become a naïve utopian project, efforts still need to be taken to control and limit the current nuclear framework through effective 'Arms control' if not disarmament. The emergence of nuclear triads – such as 'US-China-India', or 'China-India-Pakistan' – and the various indices dictating their agreements need to be re-examined and re-evaluated to deal with the current situation. In order to ensure that a workable action plan is created and followed, nations need to come together to take collective responsibility to maintain a stable and secure global environment. P5 nations should set aside their differences and involve the new NWS, since the latter are essential for the success or failure of any nuclear safety and security measures. The NPT also needs to be amended, in order to incorporate new NWS; otherwise in its current state, the treaty will become obsolete, and redundant. All nuclear and non-NWS need to comply with the legal requirements of this treaty, which is– to submit all their civilian nuclear material and facilities to safeguards. As of now, this caveat is a voluntary, non-binding measure for the Nuclear Weapon States, but this hierarchical stratification prevents a transparent and mutually beneficial process from emerging. Finally, the new NWSs also need to take responsibility and avoid callous proliferation of potentially hazardous fissile material.

The P5 nations need to step up and embrace their role in the process of creating a secure framework as it is ultimately the modernization and diversification of global missile inventories through niche technologies that is causing a cascading militarization effect in Asia. China's insecurities when faced with US modernization has led it to rapidly focus on dynamically modernizing its own military as well. This in turn has led to its rapid forays into space, via Ballistic Missile Defence programs (BMD), acquisition of MIRVs and development of Global Prompt Vehicles. These measures are threatening the precariously balanced security framework and threat perceptions in Asia as other nations within the geostrategic region are forced to re-examine their nuclear policies, in an attempt to maintain credible minimal deterrence at the very least, if not an actualized equitable power balance. If China turns its focus towards the development of Ballistic Missile Defence (BMD) technologies, its regional neighbours such as India would be forced to invest in Multiple Independently targetable Re-entry Vehicle (MIRV) and other such deterrence capable technologies in order to maintain their own domestic security framework. Therefore, more cooperative-mechanisms with additional focus on realistic targets, greater transparency and legally compliant security frameworks are required.

As far as the nuclear safeguards, security, and proliferation issues are concerned there are several treaties that try to address these issues. Treaties such as The Convention on Physical Protection of Nuclear Materials (CPPNM), United Nations Security Council Resolution

(UNSCR) 1540, International Convention for the Suppression of Acts of Nuclear Terrorism (ICSANT), are a few of the treaties that try to address these problems. But most of these treaties face certain common constraints that prevent them from effectively reorganizing the nuclear security framework. Some of these constraints are: the treaties are not universally accepted and as a result they cannot come into force; there is no mechanism to enforce the treaties or review mechanisms to monitor their implementation; and there are no prescribed punishable consequences for non-compliance. One example of this collective inefficiency is the fact that the Fissile Material Cut-off Treaty (FMCT) could not come into force, since one nation refused to sign the treaty and effectively hindered the collective process. Some researchers have avidly called for the need to place more collective sanctions on uncooperative parties as it is not merely a question of individual national interests but global interests as well. While the IAEA has a limited mandate in the area of nuclear security, this mandate is limited to civilian materials[33]. Some ways in which this inefficiency can be combated are: the regularization of all civilian nuclear power plants under the International Atomic Energy Agency (IAEA). Countries should universally enforce the Convention on Physical Protection of Nuclear Materials (CPPNM) and the countries using nuclear fissile material for military purposes, should also be monitored, because more than 90 percent of HEU is used in the military sector.

Similarly, the world's largest International Police Organization (INTERPOL), Nuclear Security Summit, Global Initiative to Combat Nuclear Terrorism (GICNT), Proliferation Security Initiative (PSI) needs to be universally accepted. Efforts should also be made towards implementing a uniform system for monitoring the enforcement of these treaties and also providing verification and assurance to other countries through external review mechanisms.[34] These measures are essential as it is important to recognize that 'Nuclear Security' is not limited to the individual interests of any one nation in particular but is a global concern with very dire consequences.

Conclusion

The nuclear explosion in 1945 catapulted the world towards a nuclear age where it was forced to face and comprehend the horrendous ill effects of the nuclear bomb. But the process also made nations world over understand, that nuclearization is not an individuated or geographically limited process but one that has global consequences that transcend boundaries. Irrespective of the scale, any nuclear catastrophe has the potential to cause tremendous chaos and endanger the entire human race. Ever since then, nations have been collectively trying to address these challenges through various disarmament and nuclear safety and security treaties, but a lot of the cooperative mechanisms happen to be slow and inconsistent. Given the current precarious scenario, nations need to rise above petty power politics and uniformly ratify regulatory mechanisms. Also, countries that support and harbor terrorist activities need to understand that terrorists that are driven solely by ideology, will stop at nothing to access these modalities of power and will capitalize on any vulnerability in security frameworks. It is an unfortunate fact, that all nations have fault lines which these non-state actors can easily exploit, which is why it is essential to take pre-emptive measures, come together in order to stop this cancerous growth, otherwise the looming threat of nuclear terrorism will strike first and lead to an apocalyptic disintegration of the human race.

Endnotes

1   Nuclear Security Fundamentals Objective and Essential Elements of a State's Nuclear Security Regime, IAEA Nuclear Security Series No. 20

2   Christopher P.Twomey,"Introduction: Dangerous Dynamism In Asia's Nuclear Future", in Roundtable, Approaching Critical Mass: Asia's Multipolar Nuclear world, National Bureau of Asian Research, at http://nbr.org/publications/asia_policy/Free/AP19/AP19_CriticalMassRT_Jan2014.pdf

3   Nuclear Power in the World Today, World Nuclear Association (Updated-February 2015), at http://www.world-nuclear.org/info/Current-and-Future-Generation/Nuclear-Power-in-the-World-Today/

4   Asia's Nuclear Energy Growth, World Nuclear Association, updated July 2015 at http://www.world-nuclear.org/info/Country-Profiles/Others/Asia-s-Nuclear-Energy-Growth/

5   Fitzpatrick Mark, 'Overcoming Pakistan's Nuclear Dangers', International Institute of Strategic Studies, Routledge Publications,2014

6   Ibid

7   International Panel on Fissile Materials, Countries, Pakistan

8   Country Profile , Pakistan, NTI athttp://www.nti.org/country-profiles/pakistan/nuclear/

9   Global Fissile Material Report 2015,IPMF, at http://fissilematerials.org/library/ipfm15.pdf

10 Fitzpatrick Mark, 'Overcoming Pakistan's Nuclear Dangers', International Institute of Strategic Studies, Routledge Publications,2014

11 Pakistan Navy Foils Terrorist Attack on Naval Base Sep. 9, 2014 ,By USMAN ANSARI   at http://archive.defencenews.com/article/20140909/DEFREG03/309090037/Pakistan-Navy-Foils-Terrorist-Attack-Naval-Base   , accessed on 20 August 2015

12 Karachi's new terrorist groups, Zia Ur Rehman, 06 January 2012, at http://www.thefridaytimes.com/beta2/tft/article.php?issue=20120106&page=5

13 Rehman Iskander, 'Murky Waters', Carnegie Endowment for International Peace,2015

14 Annual Report to Congress: Military and Security Developments Involving the People's Republic of China 2015 at http://www.defence.gov/pubs/2015_China_Military_Power_Report.pdf

15 Ibid

16 Tellis Ashley, 'China India and Pakistan-Growing Nuclear Capabilities with no End in Sight",Carnegie Endowment, 25 February 2015

17 Tellis Ashley, 'China India and Pakistan-Growing Nuclear Capabilities with no End in Sight", Carnegie Endowment, 25 February 2015

18 Nuclear Black Markets: Pakistan AQ Khan and the rise of Proliferation networks A net Assessment", IISS Strategic Dossier,2007

19 Levy and Scott-Clark, "Deception: Pakistan, the United States and the global Nuclear weapons conspiracy ",December 2005

20 Saudi nuclear weapons 'on order' from Pakistan, Mark Urban, BBC NEWS, 06 November 2013, at http://www.bbc.com/news/world-middle-east-24823846accessed on 24 September 2015

21 Ibid

22 Pakistan's nuclear-bomb maker says North Korea paid bribes for know-how,By R. Jeffrey Smith, The Washington Post, July 6, 2011,at https://www.washingtonpost.com/world/national-security/pakistans-nuclear-bomb-maker-says-north-korea-paid-bribes-for-know-how/2010/11/12/gIQAZ1kH1H_story.html

23 'The Ultimate North Korea: Nightmare Could Sell Saudi Arabia Nuclear Weapon",Zachary Keck , The National Interest, June 22, 2015,http://nationalinterest.org/feature/the-ultimate-nightmare-north-korea-could-sell-saudi-arabia-13162

24 "International Convention for the Suppression of Acts of Nuclear Terrorism ", at http://www.un.org/en/sc/ctc/docs/conventions/Conv13.pdf .

25 Bunn, Matthew, Colonel Yuri Morozov, Rolf Mowatt-Larssen, Simon Saradzhyan, William Tobey, Colonel General (ret.) Viktor I. Yesin, and Major General (ret.) Pavel S. Zolotarev (2011). "The U.S.-Russia Joint Threat Assessment on Nuclear Terrorism" (PDF).Belfer Center for Science and International Affairs, Harvard University

26 Global Fissile Material Report 2015,IPFM, at http://fissilematerials.org/library/ipfm15.pdf

27 Bunn, Matthew. "Securing the Bomb 2010: Securing All Nuclear Materials in Four Years" (PDF). President and Fellows of Harvard College.

28 Bunn, Matthew and Col-Gen. E.P. Maslin (2010). "All Stocks of Weapons-Usable Nuclear Materials Worldwide Must be Protected Against Global Terrorist Threats" (PDF). Belfer Center for Science and International Affairs, Harvard University.RetrievedJuly 26, 2012.

29 Islamic State says could Obtain Nuclear bomb in less than 12 months, at Sputnik http://sputniknews.com/middleeast/20150523/1022481189.html

30 "Islamic State Says Could Obtain Nuclear Bomb in Less Than 12 Months". Sputnik. May 23, 2015. Retrieved May 23, 2015.

31 A study by Belfer Center for Science and International Affairs at Harvard University titled "Securing the Bomb 2010

32 Could terrorists get hold of a nuclear bomb?, BBC, 2010-04-12,as stated by Rolf Mowatt-Larssen, A former investigator with the CIA and the US department of energy,athttp://news.bbc.co.uk/2/hi/americas/8615484.stm

33 Global Dialogue On Nuclear Security Priorities Nuclear Security Primer: The Existing System September 2014,NTI at http://www.nti.org/media/pdfs/Nuclear_Security_Primer_September_2014.pdf?_=1413920986

34 Ibid

Chapter Seven

Bilateral Cooperation between the ROK and India: ROK's Perspective

Park Min-hyoung, PhD
Korea National Defence University

Introduction

In 2015, the ROK and India marked the 42th anniversary of diplomatic ties.[1] In fact the relations between two states have made great strides in recent years and have become truly multi-dimensional. South Korean President Park Geun-hye visited India in 2014 and Indian Prime Minister Narendra Modi visited South Korea on May 18 2015 in order to celebrate the 70th anniversary of Korean independence from Japan. He stressed that "India considers Korea as an important partner for the modernization of the Indian economy. We are working hard to develop the trade relations with Korea" Two leaders held substantive discussion in areas of mutual interests and they agreed to upgrade the bilateral relationship to a "Special Strategic Partnership"

The relationship between two states has just focused on the economic and technology issues, because the relation is driven, in the first place, by economic considerations.[2] In the 2015 summit, the Indian Prime Minister expressed support for the ROK government's effort to build trust in the Korean Peninsula and to lay the groundwork for peaceful reunification of the Peninsula. Yet, the relation has enormous potential for further development in terms of security and military relations. In fact, for the last 60 years, maintaining a strong bilateral alliance with the United States has been the key focus of South Korea's security strategy. The alliance has been central to the national security and economic advancement of the Republic of Korea. It has played pivotal role in deterring the North Korean threat and in contributing to political and economic stability in South Korea and even Northeast Asia as a whole. The existence of North Korea as an imminent threat made the US' support indispensable for the ROK government.

In addition, the Korean Peninsula, surrounded by four major powers; the US, China, Japan and Russia, is inherently vulnerable to drastic changes in the security environment of the region. The security environment has undergone significant changes in the 60 years since the Korean War. Thus strong deterrence capability based on the ROK-US alliance has become fundamental in prohibiting a second Korean war. With this deterrence power maintaining some degree of stability, it is seen that the ROK should pursue a policy that aims to achieve peaceful unification in the future.

For peaceful and expeditious reunification, bilateral approaches between the two Koreas may be the best suited to achieving a breakthrough in the current stalemate. Considering current hostilities and confrontation between two parties, however, such an approach is more complicated than it appears. Thus, in order to establish a solid peaceful system and the peaceful unification in the Peninsula the ROK should try to broaden its policy scope and enhance international cooperation.

Unlike other regional states, South Korea does not have any reason to oppose security cooperation in the region because it cannot separate its national defence strategy from security cooperation with other states. Thus, the ROK should expand its cooperation in terms of security and defence. With this backdrop, this paper focuses on the bilateral security and defence cooperation between the ROK and India for maintaining robust security of Korean Peninsula. In particular, it will explore why the cooperation is needed between two states and what is ROK's reasonable policy direction for this cooperation.

Why the bilateral security cooperation with India is necessary for the ROK

There are various ways for states to guarantee their security. Ever since their first appearance in history, all states have continuously tried to maintain their national security. Their efforts to fulfill this objective can be divided into two methods: on the one hand, states seek to increase their own capabilities (self-help) and, on the other, states may seek to cooperate with other states. Kenneth N. Waltz, the theorist behind structural neo-realism, suggests that behaviour which is aimed at increasing the capability of a state in order to sustain its sovereignty may be termed "internal balancing," while collaborating with other states can be seen as "external balancing"[3]

Generally speaking, the term security is used in international politics and other social science disciplines in a specifically state-centric way. The term has been used loosely since World War II and has been expanded in its scope of meaning as time has gone on. There are two points of view in terms of the concept of security – one narrow and one wide.[4] The narrower interpretations of security tend to focus on military counter-activities conducted by countries against the military threats of enemy states. The wider term can also be used to describe a range of activities initiated by a government in support of the state. The concept has been expanded upon because the international security system is becoming ever more complicated and economic and social interdependence between and amongst states has dramatically increased in twenty-first century geopolitics.[5]

In the current international system, it is no longer controversial to say that there is a difference between the traditional concept of security (one focused on national military policy) and the current conceptualization of security. The threats faced within human society are becoming more multi-directional and complex than ever before.[6] As the scope of threats has broadened and incorporated transnational threats such as terrorism, weapons of mass destruction, public health issues and global ecological problems, the concept of security has begun to include the resolution of these diverse threats.[7] Robert Picciotto suggests that although military deterrence will forever be one of the crucial factors in national security strategy composition, it will not solely govern states' security policies any longer because of the multiplicity of security issues in the contemporary international context.[8] In addition, Joseph S. Nye asserts that the definition of security changes with the threats faced, and many states are equally concerned about economic, social, and environmental security as they are about military security.[9]

In short, as the international system has become more complicated and interdependence between states has gradually increased, the concept of security has concomitantly broadened, and it now comprises every governmental action in the global political system. Considering the increasing interdependence in the international arena and the fact that economic issues are crucial factors in national management and politics, a given state's unstable security situation is not just its own problem. For example, new security threats such as nuclear weapons can bring about tension in the region due to their nature of being indiscriminate, largely uncontrollable and not restricted. In this sense, the North Korean nuclear issue is not a problem for the Korean Peninsula alone, but is a Northeast Asian security and even a global issue because it is directly connected to regional and global security. Therefore, regional actors should cooperate with each other in seeking to maintain peace in the region.

In addition, currently every state focuses more on the welfare and wellbeing of human beings (its people). Thus, in the competitive environment, states seek to maximize its gains through cooperation. In Asian region, even after the Cold War, there still remained elements of instability such as on the Korean Peninsula and the Taiwan Strait. Thus, most of the states in the region have tried to increase their military capabilities and therefore are heavily armed at present. In particular, the two divided Koreas still face each other. In addition, while the concepts of the nation-state and nationalism were weakened with economic integration in Europe, there are still outstanding territorial dispute and issues between regional states. Simply put, there are still unsolved problems, different ideologies, historical antagonism, the arms race, territorial disputes, a power gap among nations in the region and issues which make it difficult to cooperate each other. Also, the current stumbling blocks, as explained above, cannot be removed easily.

However, it does not mean that security cooperation is impossible. For instance, when Japanese Prime Minister, Abe Shinzo, denied official involvement in the "comfort women" controversy, South Korea and China criticized his statement by emphasizing that "responsible leaders of Japan should have a correct understanding of history" and "Japan should face up to history and take responsibility." However, official meetings between the states did not stop as a result of Abe's statements because South Korea and China did not want to jeopardize their national interest due to 'anti-Japanism'. In other words, regional states are attaching importance to cooperation with neighboring states.

The ROK and India are also sharing security concern emerging from the rise of China, even amidst common economic interests. China has demonstrated its intention to challenge the US-led international and regional order. Thus the US-China rivalry would grow and the Asian paradox would also be strengthened. China's key national interests in the 21st century can be defined in the following four directions: 1) guaranteeing national security and unity and achieving national economic development and prosperity; 2) defending against external aggression and protecting territorial sea and air and international borders; 3) deterring Taiwan's independence and other separatist activities and suppressing all forms of terrorism and extremism; and 4) creating a security environment conducive to the development of national peace. China's Defence White Paper defined the current period as China's strategic opportunity for national progress and emphasized the awareness of its role in the new multipolar international order. It expresses China's self-confidence as a superpower and calls for the modernization of its military power and development of science on the basis of its economic growth.

China's military policies are currently aimed at coping with the growth of Japanese military power, curbing the U.S. military influence in Asia and safeguarding its national interests in view of future security threats such as the Taiwan issue. Since the middle of the 1980s, China has cut back its military manpower by a total of 1.5 million on two occasions, and in 2005 reduced its military strength by another 200,000 men. It has established yet another plan to further reduce 300,000 troops by 2015 as the military shifts to a more technology-intensive structure. Over the past several years, China has made efforts to acquire a core strategic weapons system which includes nuclear submarines, long-range strategic weapons and aircraft carriers, already exhibiting some concrete outcomes.[10]

There is already substantial evidence that Asian states are worried about China's ascendancy and have moved to contain it.[11] It is under these circumstances that , the ROK and India are pursuing to develop its economic and security relations concurrently. Without cooperation among the regional states, peace and prosperity cannot be achieved.[12] That is why the bilateral security cooperation between two states is necessary in terms of security.

The Relations between the ROK and India

Relations between Korea and India stretch back to 48AD, when an Indian princess is said to have come to Korea from the historical city of Ayodhya in India, and, after marring King Kim-Suro, came to be known as Queen Hur Hwang-ok.[13] However, it is unfortunate that the two countries only established consular relations in 1962, in spite of the long association between their people.

The last seventy years have witnessed many changes in the relations between the ROK and India. Despite the development of the ROK-India relations in the immediate aftermath of World War, the relations between the two countries did not develop further and remained minimal throughout the Cold war period. However, there has been a rapid improvement in the relations from 1991 to 2009, and the deepening of the relations from 2010 to 2015.

In fact, the diplomatic ties between the two states formally established in 1973. Since then, two states' cooperation normally has focused on economic relations. Several trade agreements have been signed, Agreement on Trade Promotion and Economic and Technological Co-operation in 1974; Agreement on Co-operation in Science & Technology in 1976; Convention on Double Taxation Avoidance in 1985 (which revised in 2015[14]) and Bilateral Investment Promotion/Protection Agreement in 1996. Due to these Agreements, the volume of trade between the ROK and India has increased substantially, exemplified by growth from mere $530 million in 1992, to $10 billion in 2006, and to $17.6 billion in the year 2013.

However, during the Cold war, the bilateral relation was limited by the international political system. In other words, while India ended up with supporting Soviet Union's policies in Asia, the ROK had maintained a strong alliance with the United States and supported its action in Asia. This dichotomy made it difficult for two states to maintain close relationship even though they had some economy-related agreements. In addition, two states showed almost no interest in developing economic relations with each other because they had different economic systems.

From 1991 to 2009, the relations between two states had developed rapidly, because the huge obstacle, Cold war, was eliminated. In other words, the end of the Cold War and the emergence of a new post-Cold war system in the region paved the way for the opening a new era in the ROK-India relations. South Korea tried to seize this new political and economic opportunities. In September 1993, Indian Prime Minster PV Narasimha Rao visited the ROK in the first ever visit of an Indian Prime Minister to Korea. In 1996, South Korea President Kim Young-sam went to India and two states agreed to set-up a Joint Commission at the Foreign Ministers levels for bilateral cooperation.

In addition, India changed its policy direction from the import substitution industrialization policy to an economic liberalization policy, and the ROK tried to finding a new market for its developing economy. As the Indian economy grew, more and more people were being elevated to the middle-class, thereby creating a huge market for Korean Companies. These changes caused both state's policymaker to recognize each other's value. As seen in Table 1, the trade volume (ROK's export to India) between two states increased 17 times. Moreover, in terms of politics, India tilted towards the ROK, compared with the Cold war period when it inclined rather towards North Korea- than the South. In 2004, Long Term Cooperative Partnership between two states was established when President Roh Moo-hyun visited India. It was an actual beginning of political relations between two states. In other words, this served as bedrock of the bilateral relations.[15]

Table 1 ROK's Trade with India, 1991-2009

Year	Total Ex.	Ex. to India	Rate (%)	Total Im.	Im. to India	Rate (%)
1991	71,870,122	468,669	0.6	81,524,858	484,846	0.6
1995	125,057,988	1,125,814	1.0	135,118,933	798,297	0.6
2000	172,267,510	1,326,166	0.8	160,481,018	984,706	0.6
2005	284,418,743	4,597,837	1.6	261,238,264	2,112,076	0.8
2009	363,533,561	8,013,290	2.2	323,084,521	4,141,622	1.3

Source: The Korea International Trade Association

Since 2010, the two state's relation has been deepening further. South Korean president Lee Myung-bak visited India as the chief guest on the occasion of the 61st Republic Day celebrations in January 2010. That was a landmark visit in the history of the ROK-India relations as the bilateral ties were elevated the level of strategic partnership for the long-term cooperative partnership for peace and prosperity.[16] In July 2011, another milestone was achieved during the state visit of the India president Pratibha Patil to the ROK. In March 2012, the then prime minister Manmohan Singh visited South Korea to participate in the Nuclear Security Summit, and in January 2014, ROK president Park Geun-hye visited - India.[17] President Park was accompanied by a business delegation, and the main highlight was a memorandum of understanding signed between 'The Export-Import Bank of Korea' and 'India Infrastructure Finance Co Ltd' for the funding of infrastructure project. And, South Korea's strategic initiatives in East Asia, among them trust-building on the Korean Peninsula and the Northeast Asia Peace and Cooperation Initiative were discussed.[18]

India also regards the ROK as a strategic partner for its economy and security. Indian Prime Minister expressed his views on the ROK as follows; "the ROK's transformation and its emergence as a vibrant democracy, one of the fastest growing economies in the world and a powerhouse of innovation in just two generations is an inspiration for the whole of Asia." That means the ROK could be central to India's Look East Policy[19]

Two state's relation has been evolved since 2010 as mentioned above. And, this trend might continue for the time being because two states share common economic interests. And, the convergence of common democratic values has brought two states closer to each other.[20] Also, they have significant political factor, the emergence a multipolar system in Asia, which cause to deepen the relation. Thus, two states have to expand its security relation to prepare for security environment that is changing drastically in Asia.

Table 2 High Level Visit from the ROK to India

Year	Dates and Visitors
1990	March, Foreign Minister Mr. Choi Ho-joong
1991	January, Speaker of the National Assembly Mr. Park Jun-kyu
1994	September, Minister of Commerce Mr. Kim Chul-soo
1996	February, President Mr. Kim Young-sam
1999	February, Prime Minister Mr. Kim Jong-pil
2000	July, Foreign Minister Mr. Lee Joung-bin
2001	July, Minister of Information and Communication Mr. Yang Seung-taek
2002	April, Minister of Information and Communication Mr. Yang Seung-taek
2003	December, Foreign Minister Mr. Yoon Young-kwan

Year	Dates and Visitors
2004	October, RoK President Mr. Roh Moo-hyun
2005	August, Foreign Minister Mr. Ban Ki-moon
2006	November, Minister of Commerce, Industry and Energy Mr. Chung Se-kyun May, Deputy Prime Minister & Finance Minister Mr. Han Duk-soo
2007	April, Foreign Minister Mr. Song Min-soon
2008	May, Defence Minister Mr. Kim Jang-soo
2009	June, Minister of Foreign Affairs and Trade Mr. Yu Myung-hwan
2010	24-27 January, President of ROK Mr. Lee Myung-bak
2011	September, Chairman of Defence Acquisition Program Administration Mr. Noh Dae-lae July, Minister of Land Transport and Maritime Affairs Mr. Kwon Do-youp May, Chairman of National Defence Committee Mr. Won Yoo-chul 21 April, Chancellor, Institute of Foreign Affairs and National Security Mr. Lee Joon-gyu March, Minister of Justice Mr. Lee Kwi-nam 22-26 March, Speaker of National Assembly Mr. Park Hee-tae 20 January, Minister for Trade Mr. Kim Jong-hoon 17 January, Minister of Strategy and Finance Mr. Yoon, Jeung-hyun

Year	Dates and Visitors
2012	27-28 June, First Vice Minister of Foreign Affairs Mr. Ahn Ho-young
	28 July, Chief Election Commissioner Justice Mr. Kim Nung Hwan
	16-17 September, Minister of Strategy & Finance Mr. Bahk Jaewan
	8-19 October, Vice-Minister of Environment Mr. Yoon, Jong-soo
	28 Nov.-01 Dec, Minister of Defence Mr. Kim, Kwan-jin
	11-12 Dec, Minister of Education, Science & Technology Mr. Lee Ju-Ho
	13 December, Minister of Culture, Sports & Tourism Mr. Choe Kwang-sik
2013	8 November, Minister of Foreign Affairs Mr. Yun Byung-se
	26 -29 January, Minister of Knowledge Economy Dr. Hong Sukwoo
2014	15 – 18 January, President of the Republic of Korea Madame Park Geun-hye
	15 – 18 January, Minister of Foreign Affairs Mr. Yun Byung-se
	15- 18 January, Minister of Science, ICT and Future Planning Dr. Choi Mun-Kee
	8 January, Deputy Prime Minister and Minister of Strategy and Finance Dr. Hyun, Oh-seok
2015	12-15 March, Mr. Suh Byung-soo, Mayor of Busan to India
	7-10May, Mr. Chung Ui-hwa, Speaker of National Assembly of ROK to India
	23-28 August, Mr. Shin Dong-bin, Chairman, Lotte Group to India

Source: Embassy of India in Seoul.

How the Cooperation could be expanded: The ROK's perspective

In the time that international terrorism and nuclear proliferation have become the dominant security concerns in international community, to achieve peaceful unification in the Peninsula as Germany did in the late 20th century is one of the most central goals of South Korea. In spite of the economic crisis and sanction from the international community, North Korea is still developing its nuclear weapons. Thus the nuclear problem of North Korea received the utmost attention from the globe. To solve the North Korean nuclear issues and achieve peaceful process and unification, these efforts should be continued in the international cooperation. Of course, some take a skeptical view of the cooperation. For example neo-realists examine the issues of cooperation from the point of view of the distribution of power and the concept of relative gain. Accordingly, for neo-realists, the factors of anarchy, uncertainty, and survival strongly affect states' actions in the process of cooperation. Glenn Snyder asserts that "even when no state has any desire to attack others, none can be sure that others' intentions are peaceful, or will remain so; hence each must accumulate power for defence"[21]. Thus, they strongly asserted that cooperation between states might be impossible and that although cooperation can occur in the international system, it is very difficult for all members to obtain their goals and, therefore, it is more difficult to maintain cooperation. Waltz explains the difficulty in keeping international institutions as follows:[22]

> States cannot entrust managerial powers to a central agency unless that agency is able to protect its client states. The more powerful the clients and the more the power of each of them appear as a threat to the others, the greater the power lodged in the center must be. The greater the power of the center, the stronger the incentive for states to engage in a struggle to control it.

However, major regional states have experienced the use of cooperation in resolving regional issues and it is clear that peaceful way is better than the forceful one to resolve the security issues. For this, South Korea must continuously expand its security cooperation to actively take part in making a peaceful process in the Peninsula. Simply put, the ROK has to maintain its relationship with Asian states robustly, because their political, diplomatic and military support is an indispensable factor for its security and economy. South Korea could expand its relationship with them by strengthening its bilateral relationship. Thus, South Korea has to emphasize the global benefits the unification could bring. In addition, South Korea has to convince the regional actors including India that the North Korean nuclear issue is not only a problem for the Korean Peninsula but an Asian security issue, because it is directly connected to the regional security, and therefore, regional actors should cooperate with each other to maintain peace in Northeast Asia. Also, it has to assert that the region needs to escape from the Hobbesian idea of viewing the other as enemy and embrace the Kantian ideal of viewing the others as friend.

In this way India could be one of the good partners because, as mentioned above, two states has common economic and security interests. To enhance cooperation between the ROK and India, there are a number of suggestions that two states might consider. In this paper three major suggestions are presented in the level of strategic partnership.

Firstly, two states have to strengthen economic tie because it will give a strong foundation for security cooperation by increasing interdependence between two states. For the ROK, India is of considerable economic and geopolitical significance. Under the new Indian government which make easier access do business together, a number of Korean companies will be investing in India's future by building factories, transferring commercial technology, and generating more local employment. In terms of economy, India, post reforms of its market system, is an emerging growth market. It also could be a bridge for ROK's business to penetrate the Middle East and African market considering its long and historical engagement with these two regions. In addition, the ROK can also benefit from science and technology cooperation with India. India has strength in the software industry, and the ROK has competitiveness in hardware. Thus if two states have cooperated in this domain, it could bring very efficient and successful outcomes.

For India, the ROK can be an attractive partner for cooperation because it can help to modernize India's social infrastructure such as road, railways. Also, the ROK is the fifth largest source of investment in India. In the report researched by the Goldman Sachs, "How India Can Become the Next Korea", it suggested that India should adopt the Korean Model to boost its manufacturing, considering a remarkable resemblance between the current Indian economy and the South Korean economy of the 1970s. South Korea and India already signed a Comprehensive Economic Partnership Agreement (CEPA) in 2010, setting up a major framework for further boosting bilateral trade investment ties. The CEPA is the first deal of its kind which India signed with an OECD country and South Korea with a BRIC nation. However it can still hardly be said that it works properly to maximize it economic cooperation. Thus, two governments should encourage more aggressive investment in partner's economy.[23] In that sense, to form Free Trade Agreement is one of the best options to increase its economic tie.

Secondly, it should increase direct and indirect security cooperation. India is an emerging global power and it can contribute to ensuring stability in Asia and it could play an important and positive role in the process of resolving security issues in the Korean Peninsula. In fact, two states have established a Foreign Policy and Security Dialogue (FPSD) at Secretary (Vice-Ministerial) level, which last met at New Delhi on 28 June 2012, two states have a regular dialogue between the two Ministries of Defence. The first ever such Defence Policy Dialogue (DPD) at the level of a Deputy Minister of the Ministry of Defence was held at Seoul on 24 December 2013 followed by the second at Delhi on 20 January 2015. In 2014 summit, President Park Geun-hye and Prime Minister Narendra Modi agreed to pursue mutually beneficial defence industry cooperation and prepared to established military confidence by concluding a General Security of Military Information Agreement (GSOMIA).[24] Moreover, India is the only country with which South Korea maintains a security dialogue besides it four neighboring power – the US, China, Japan, and Russia. In addition, between Defence Research and Development Organization (DRDO) of India and Defence Acquisition Programme Administration (DAPA) MOUs were signed to enhance defence cooperation. Also, as India is one of the biggest arms importers in the world, there are ample opportunities for Korean weapons manufacturers to sell their products to India.

Thus, the ROK will continuously pursue the exchanges of senior-level officials and regular meeting with India. However, in order to increase bilateral defence and security cooperation between two states, it is necessary that the level of dialogue has to be upgraded. That means two states have to conduct regular defence dialogue with Minister-level. By doing so, the defence and security cooperation could be deepened and expanded. In addition, two states should substantially increase exchange of military officers. It does not mean days-stay visit, but years-stay visit or for courses. It will contribute toward greater interaction and understanding between the two militaries.

Thirdly, it should enhance cultural exchange. In March 2012, in order to improve people-to-people ties an agreement on visa simplification was signed. The two states signed a MoU to enhance bilateral air service cooperation and they also agreed to open more destinations for airlines on both sides, apart from increase in frequencies, in October 2015.[25] That means the road to increase personal exchanges are being paved. It will strengthen identity-bonding between two states. In fact, an Indian Culture Center was established in ROK in April 2011 and the Festival of India was inaugurated on 30 June 2011. In autumn of 2015, India sent a full Festival of India, and South Korea will host a Festival of Korea in India in 2016. Indian Community in the ROK is estimated to be about 8,000 people including businessmen, IT professionals, scientists, research fellows, students and workers. Two states should intensify to exchange young generation, because it will give an opportunity to encourage greater understanding and interaction between the future leaders of the two states.

Conclusion

North Korean threat is still serious to South Korea, because it has a series of asymmetric capabilities and it can cause severe damage to South Korean society, although any invasion would not be fully successful. Thus, South Korea needs to keep its security stable through the ROK-

US alliance, and through cooperation with other states. In this regards, the India is an attractive partner in security cooperation, because India is a growing power in Asian region and it could play a positive role to mitigate tension on the Peninsula, even in the process of reunification. Of course, for India, it is necessary to check the Islamabad -Pyongyang relationship by strengthening the ROK-India security cooperation.

It is true that cooperation between states could face some problems because international system is anarchic and each state may act according to its own self-interests. However, we have a tendency to underestimate the role of international economic processes, and interactions among states which have a strong effect on a state's behavior. ROK-India bilateral relations are important both from a security and economic perspective. Especially, in terms of economy and technology, two states relationship has proven beneficial in many areas. Prime Minister Modi's vision to turn India into a global manufacturing hub, called "Make in India" initiative aims to attract foreign capital through business-friendly policies. And, India has an immense market of over 1.3 billion people. Thus, two states economic cooperation which pivots on ROK's capital and India's market has significant potential for each other.

In spite of active economic cooperation, it is true that the political and security dimension of the ROK-India cooperation remains underdeveloped. It's time to expand this to security and defence area. During Indian Prime Minister Narendra Modi's visit to Seoul in May 2015, two states signed a Special Strategic Partnership agreement reflecting mutual aspirations for broad-based cooperation. Considering current changing security environment, Seoul and New Delhi could be ideal partners in terms of security. Simply put, two states should strengthen a security and economic relationship at the same time because two states share numerous strategic interests. For example, China's recent aggressive action to deal with certain territorial disputes rapidly changes its "peaceful rise" image. In this context, the ROK-India security and military cooperation has much more potential than expected. It is the robust security relations with India, which is in the process of transforming itself from an elephant into lion,[26]that could help the ROK get its supporter in the process of reunification and consolidate its position in East Asia.

Endnotes

1 In this research, the terms "Republic of Korea" and "South Korea" are all used interchangeably

2 Rajiv Sikri, "India's Look East Policy," Asia-Pacific Review, Vol. 16, No. 1(2009), p. 132

3 Kenneth N. Waltz, *Theory of International Politics* (California: Addison-Wesley, 1979), p. 168.

4 Barry Buzan et al., *Security: A New Framework for Analysis* (Boulder: Lynne Reiner, 1998). They explained these two views of security as the new one of the wideners and the old military and state-centered view of the traditionalists.

5 Ken Booth, *Critical Security Studies and World Politics* (London: Lynne Rienner, 2005).

6 Ken Booth suggested the sources of threats in details; "globalization, population growth, extremist ideologies, apparently unstoppable technological momentum, terrorism, consumerism, tyranny, massive disparities of wealth, rage, imperialism, nuclear-biological-chemical weapons and brute capitalism." For details, see Ken Booth, *Critical Security Studies and World Politics* (London: Lynne Rienner, 2005).

7 G. J. Ikenberry and A. Moravcsik, Liberal Theory and the Politics of Security in Northeast Asia, *Paper Prepared for the Ford Foundation Project on Non-Traditional Security* (2006), p. 13.

8 R. Picciotto, "Why the World Needs Security Goals", *Conflict Secuirty & Development*, Vol. 6, No. 1 (2006), p. 114. He showed eight millennium security goals citing United Nations' report: 1) Reduce conflict between and within states, 2) Promote nuclear, radiological, chemical, and biological disarmament, 3) Design and implement a collective strategy against terrorism, 4) Combat transnational organized crime, 5) Implement and enforce effective sanctions to protect human security, 6) Authorize the use of force, based on agreed criteria, 7) Strengthen peace enforcement, peacekeeping, and peace building and protect civilians, 8) Reform the United Nations to meet the challenges of human security.

9 Joseph S. Nye, *Understanding International Conflicts*, 6th Edition (New York: Addison Wesley Longman, 2007), p. 9.

10 Park Min-hyoung, "The Rise of China and Korea's Military Strategic Choice," *Journal of International Studies*, Vol. 52, No. 1(2012).

11 John Mearsheimer, "Can China Rise Peacefully?" *National Interest* (October 14, 2014).

12 Many theorists suggest that powerful Asian states including the ROK and India are likely to join the hand to balance against China's rising power. For more details, see Stephen Walt, "Balancing Act," Foreign Policy (May 3, 2010).

13 Kim Byoung-Mo, *Hur Hwang-Ok Route From India to Gaya* (Seoul: Morning of History, 2008), p. 238.

14 The purpose of The ROK-India Double Taxation Avoidance Convention is to avoid the burden of double taxation on taxpayers in the two countries.

15 Rajaram Panda, "India and South Korea Relations: Past and Future Trends-Analysis," *Eurasia Review*, October 7th (2012).

16 During ROK's President Lee Myoung-bak's visit, Indian Prime Minister Manmohan Singh said that "we are delighted that a friend of India is at the helm of affairs in Korea and that together we will have the opportunity to realize our common vision of a strong and vibrant India-Korea partnership.... We are committed to developing a robust and comprehensive framework for strategic engagement with Korea."

17 Rahul Mishra, "Major defence deals on PM's agenda in South Korea," *Rediff.com*, 18th May 2015.

18 Tridivesh Singh Maini, "The Significance of Modi's South Korea Visit," *The Diplomat*, May 16th 2015.

19 Rajiv Kumar, "The Evolution of the India-South Korea Relations: A Neoclassical Realist Analysis," PhD these Sungkyunkwan Univ. (2015), p.138.

20 Singh Lakhvinder, "The Importance of South Korea: a strategic perspective on India's engagement with North Korea," Korean Journal of Defence Analysis, Vol. 20, No. 3 (2008)

21 G. H. Snyder, "The Security Dilemma in Alliance Politics," World Politics (1984), pp. 461-495.

22 Kenneth N Waltz, Theory of International Politics (California: Addison-Wesley, 1979), p.112.

23 Korean companies have invested nearly $2.93 billion up until September 2013 while Indian investment in South Korea stood at nearly $3 billion.

24 ROK MND, 2014 Defence White Paper (Seoul: MND, 2014), p. 135.

25 *The Indian Express*, "More Flights between India and Korea," 14th November 2015.

26 Elephant means large in size and slow in its gait, and lion symbolizes power, courage, strength, agility and wisdom.

References

Barry Buzan et al., *Security: A New Framework for Analysis* (Boulder: Lynne Reiner, 1998).

John Mearsheimer, "Can China Rise Peacefully?" *National Interest* (October 14, 2014).

Joseph S. Nye, *Understanding International Conflicts*, 6th Edition (New York: Addison Wesley Longman, 2007)..

Ken Booth, *Critical Security Studies and World Politics* (London: Lynne Rienner, 2005).

Kenneth N. Waltz, *Theory of International Politics* (California: Addison-Wesley, 1979).

G. J. Ikenberry and A. Moravcsik, Liberal Theory and the Politics of Security in Northeast Asia, *Paper Prepared for the Ford Foundation Project on Non-Traditional Security* (2006).

Park Min-hyoung, "The Rise of China and and Korea's Military Strategic Choice," *Journal of International Studies*, Vol. 52, No. 1(2012).

R. Picciotto, "Why the World Needs Security Goals", *Conflict Secuirty & Development*, Vol. 6, No. 1 (2006).

Rajaram Panda, "India and South Korea Relations: Past and Future Trends-Analysis," *Eurasia Review*, October 7th (2012).

Rajiv Sikri, "India's Look East Policy," Asia-Pacific Review, Vol. 16, No. 1(2009).

Rahul Mishra, "Major defence deals on PM's agenda in South Korea," *Rediff.com*, 18th May 2015.

Singh Lakhvinder, "The Importance of South Korea: a strategic perspective on India's engagement with North Korea," Korean Journal of Defence Analysis, Vol. 20, No. 3 (2008).

Snyder, G. H. "The Security Dilemma in Alliance Politics," *World Politics* (1984).

Stephen Walt, "Balancing Act," Foreign Policy (May 3, 2010).

Tridivesh Singh Maini, "The Significance of Modi's South Korea Visit," *The Diplomat*, May 16th (2015).

Rajiv Kumar, "The Evolution of the India-South Korea Relations: A Neoclassical Realist Analysis," PhD thesis Sungkyunkwan Univ. (2015).

ROK MND, 2014 Defence White Paper (Seoul: MND, 2014).

Chapter Eight

India South Korea Relations — An Indian Perspective

MH Rajesh

Early Links between India and Republic of Korea (RoK)

Introduction. Relations between any two nations are shaped by several factors. Salient ones are geographical location, history, economic relations, people to people contact, overall geopolitical context and political outlook of both nations. India-RoK relations have highly favourable elements in each of these factors. This paper attempts to discuss some of these factors that shape the bilateral relations. There are historic connections between India and RoK that goes back to 2000 years. Legend has it that Queen Suriratna /Hur Hwang-ok of Korea, of prominent lineage, came from the state of Ayodhya in India in AD48. Chronologically, the Buddhist connections provided the *next* strong foundations in the relationship. Just as Buddhism spread from India, there were Buddhist monks from Korea who visited India and added awareness and transmitted values between both countries from their travelogues, interactions and accounts. The search for more recent cultural ties between India and RoK would lead to India's prominent poet, Rabindranath Tagore who described Korea as a *'Lamp of the East'* in 1929. This has become the watchword of India's relations with Korea. Seoul has recently honoured the poet by allocating space for a statue of Tagore in Seoul[1]. Queen Suri, Buddhism and Tagore's description provide a strong cultural basis for India-RoK pre independent relations.

Post-Independence Relations. When trade has been the overt driver of relations, a salient symbolic driver of relations between India and RoK, post-independence, has been Democracy. The Chairman of UN commission to assist Korean elections in 1947 was an Indian Diplomat, KPS Menon[2]. The period after independence was followed by the Korean War, when the initial defence relations between India and RoK commenced. There were two distinct aspects to this during the Korean War. First was a humanitarian aspect, where the 60th Field Ambulance unit of Indian Army with 346 soldiers distinguished itself credibly by serving Korean People[3], performing approximately 2324 surgeries, treating 20000 in-patients and 195000[4] out-patients. These are the foundations of current people to people contact between RoK and India. Humanitarian interventions forge far deeper friendships than what diplomats, scholars and soldiers can, due to the nature of human suffering. Some of it gets reflected and picked out by media[5] from sporadic events such as a group of elderly Korean veterans seen supporting India in a small town sporting event symbolising deep people to people contact. The second aspect is that at the end of the Korean War, the Neutral Nations Repatriation Committee (NNRC) that oversaw the post war repatriation was headed by an Indian General, Thimayya. He later became a widely respected Chief of the Indian Army. 5000 soldiers from India formed the Indian Custodial Force (ICF), which enabled the process of repatriation. Given the nature of the task, scholars concede that the NNRC and ICF had a difficult task at hand, which they completed in the given period[67].

Diplomatic Relations. The Indo RoK relations evolved into a diplomatic one in 1962 with opening of consulates in both countries. The relations were raised to Ambassador level in 1973. The period between establishment of full-fledged diplomatic relations in 1973 and the end of cold war in 1989 was a difficult stage in this relation. Indian Policy of Non Alignment, RoK's alignment with the USA, India's dependence on USSR for several technological and military needs provided a very difficult setting for India-RoK relations to flourish. Though India was non-aligned, RoK considered India close to the Soviets. The initial Indian Policy was also to have an equidistant relation with DPRK and RoK. However this changed by the mid-eighties towards a favourable posture towards RoK.[8] That is also the time when Pakistan-DPRK relations gathered steam. Today, the Indo-RoK relations have evolved to a *Special Strategic Relation*. The prime facilitators of this strategic shift are shared value of democracy and the high levels of trade and commerce that thrive between India and South Korea.

India and RoK –Historic Congruence

India and RoK -Striking Similarities. A discernible feature of India and RoK relations is the striking similarities between both countries with respect to the events that both countries have faced. A few of them are elaborated below:-

- **Imperial Legacies.** India and RoK were both under imperialist rule. India was under British Rule till 1947 and Korea was under Japanese occupation till 1945. Both countries became independent at around the same time. Independence also split the countries into two parts. The Indian partition happened along with independence. A little later, after the Korean War, which was more a result of external power politics, Korea was partitioned into North and South Korea. If Indian 'partition' happened due to British divide and rule policy, in case of Korea the division of the country into two halves was more due to external ideological factors than any internal schisms.

- **Difficult Neighbourhoods.** As a result of partition, both countries inherited extremely difficult neighbours. The security challenges faced by both nations are quite similar with proxy wars by Pakistan in the case of India and deniable military operations by DPRK in the case of RoK. Both DPRK and Pakistan possess nuclear capabilities. DPRK and Pakistan have also colluded extensively with DPRK bartering Missile technology for Uranium enrichment technology from Pakistan. China played a key role in nuclearizing both these countries. Coincidentally, as this paper is being prepared in August 2015, both DPRK and Pakistan have commenced a series of violations on the border, including use of artillery, after a long hiatus.

- **Synchronised Growth.** The comparisons also extend to the fact that both nations underwent deep policy changes around the same period- the late 1980's and early 1990's. Just as India started to *'look east'*, and liberalise its economy, RoK ushered in democracy to its system adding yet another tandem step in the long list of parallels between the countries. RoK was also the first country to have taken the right risks by investing deeply in India, and thereby reaping the benefits as the first mover. At certain points of history both countries had highly complementary needs which accentuated the relation. Credit is indeed due to those who shaped policy in that period, for rightly synergising complementarity that existed during that period. End of the cold war, shared values of democracy, India's economic liberalisation, a large market in India, RoK's enviable manufacturing capability and a shared concern for security has taken the relations step by step on a positive trajectory. Few nations have achieved such a large synchronisation in their bilateral relations in such a short time.

India and RoK- People to People Ties

Korean Cultural waves in India. How the citizens of a nation perceive another nation matters a lot in bilateral relations. Popular culture plays a very important role. The recent influence of Korean culture across the globe popularly called the *Hallyu* or the *Korean Wave* is an example of Korean 'soft power'. However, from Indo-Korean perspective, this phenomenon can be divided into three different wavelets in India, which preceded the present global wave.

- First was a result of the sports diplomacy that RoK is now famous for. RoK hosted the Asiad in 1986 and Olympics in 1988 at Seoul. Around that time television foot print in India was at a point of inflection. Colour televisions had become ubiquitous and had penetrated the middle class to a high degree. This made RoK and Seoul a household name in India. The young minds which saw the Seoul spectacle today are in positions of power, and they carry a positive impression of the country. This could be counted as the first Korean wave in India.

- The second *Korean Wave* occurred with the liberalisation of markets with opening up of Indian Economy in 1990's. This was a commercial, yet popular wave when all the three chaebols of Korea, namely Samsung, Hyundai and LG commenced operation in India, gathering a very huge share of white goods markets. The Indian Middle class got true value of money with Korean products as much the Korean *Chaebols* benefitted with a growing market in India. Those young minds, who were inspired by the first wave described in the paper, by then, had grown up to ride the second wave of cars, and white goods. The high level of market share enjoyed by Korean Brands such as Hyundai, LG and Samsung is symbolic of the trust Korean brands have earned in India. A Korean Ambassador had described the ubiquitous nature of Korean white goods in Indian households as 'Ghar Ghar Ki Kahani'[9] (a hindi expression that roughly translates as the 'story in every home').

- From an Indo Korean perspective, the present global Korean Wave is a third wave termed *Hallyu* typified by its most known face- Psy. *Gangnam Style* was the staple in every social event. Korean TV serials and pop music is extremely popular in the North East of India[10], so is the case with Kerala, at the Southern tip of India where it enjoys deep following.[11] The Festival of India was held in Korea in autumn of 2015. India will host a Festival of Korea in India in 2016 taking the cultural influences further.

- Culture has also spread as collaterals effects of commerce and trade. Hyundai's presence has lead Chennai University to teach Korean Language and culture. There are around 8000 Korean Expats in India of which 3000 are in Chennai. There are Korean entertainment centres, cultural centres, churches and eateries in Chennai where they are the largest expatriate community[12].

Economic Relations

Indo RoK-Trade. Trade is a significant driver of bilateral relations. South Korea was one of the first countries to take the risk and invest in India when it started opening up its economy through the process termed *liberalisation.* In 1991, when India opened up its economy, the bilateral trade stood at 0.55 bn US $. Today the trade has touched 17bn US$ (2013), with India being the 15th largest trade partner of Korea. The India RoK trade had even briefly overtaken India's trade with Japan at 20bn US $, in 2011[13]. However, the share that India enjoys in Korea's trade stands only at 1.83%. This has a positive connotation. Being very low at 1.83%, it leaves a very large scope for improvement as the potential exists for increasing bilateral trade, which can in turn drive other aspects of the relation. There is also a case of trade surplus in favour of Korea today -at 5bn US $, it is a trend that has only increased overtime. Indian exports are mostly raw materials with Naphtha occupying 42%, whereas India imports high value products like smart phones and auto mobile parts. As far as investments go, Indian industrial houses have invested around 3bn in in South Korea[14] with Tata investing in Tata-Daewoo motors, Mahindra in Ssangyong Motors and Birla in Novelis-a chemical enterprise. This equals Korean FDI in India by the three *Chaebols* of Korea, Hyundai, LG and Samsung. The largest investment by a Korean firm is the 12 bn US $ plan by POSCO- The Pohang Steel Company. This was for an integrated steel plant in Odisha, the Eastern coastal State of India. The project faced environmental troubles, which are now under resolution. POSCO however has also a facility in Pune, where they manufacture galvanised steel plates for automotive and white goods industry.

Comprehensive Economic Cooperation Agreement or CEPA. Identifying commerce and economics as a driver of the relation, a fillip to this aspect was given by the Comprehensive Economic Cooperation Agreement or CEPA between India and RoK in 2010. This is the first South Korean free trade agreement with a BRIC nation. The aim of this agreement is to stream line tariffs from existing thousands to just six lines of tariffs. It also aims at reducing the trade deficit. Most Agriculture products are not included in this tariff reduction, which explains part of trade deficit. India is still an agricultural based economy which gets adversely affected by a stringent policy against agriculture products. The Korean side has indicated that IT, Generic Medicines and textiles is an area that can close this trade imbalance [15] The CEPA has also opened up services sector, which is one of India's strengths, albeit to a limited extant. Man power is another area, where India can contribute- as an ageing population in Korea will require people. The year CEPA was established the trade increased by 40%. Despite this it needs to address the bilateral trade more effectively. The Joint statement between India and RoK after the 2015 summit has indicated that the India and RoK will amend CEPA by June 2016 with an aim of achieving qualitative and quantitative increase of trade through an agreed roadmap.

Economic Relations-Beyond Indian Markets. India not only serves as a market, it also serves as the manufacturing hub for some of the Korean Manufacturing giants (Chaebols). Hyundai manufactures 600000 cars in its Chennai Plant and exports 230000 cars to 120 countries from India[16] with 90% localised products. This is a model that can be emulated by other industries in Korea, argues analyst Soyen Park in the Diplomat, articulating that India can be a manufacturing hub and a 'bridge' between RoK and its markets in Middle East and Africa[17]. Hyundai presently has 20% market share in Indian automobile industry[18]. With predicted growth of Indian middle class, this share is likely to grow in the future. The Hyundai model of using India as the base is the basis of *Make In India*- our new catch phrase for economic development. RoK has also extended US $10 bn for mutual cooperation in infrastructure, comprising Economic Development Cooperation Fund (US $ 1 billion) and export credits (US $ 9 billion) for priority sectors, including smart cities, railways, power generation and transmission. This is extremely critical to India which envisages a requirement of 1 tn US $ in investment in the next five years. This adds to mitigate the huge infrastructure funding gap in Asia which requires 8tn US$ in the next ten years[19].

Emerging Areas

The Emerging Areas -Maritime Content. The recent visit by Prime Minister Modi also highlighted 'maritime content' in the Indo Korean relationship, when he visited the Hyundai Heavy Industries. A case in point is Korean Expertise in building specialised ships, such as LNG Carriers which are crucial to energy security. India has abundant natural gas across its neighbourhood, however, they are mired in pipeline politics of the troubled AfPak region. LNG carriers are the option when pipelines get tangled in politics. Therefore there is a high complementarity between India's *need* and RoKs *expertise* in specialised shipbuilding. A Joint Working Group has been setup with a MoU in this regard. This aims at cooperation for stable maritime transport, possible joint business projects in the area of shipping and logistics, and promotion of employment of both countries' seafarers. India has just launched a project called the Sagarmala[20], which is aimed at development of maritime infrastructure along the coasts including ports, inland waterways, ship building and coastal shipping. With "Make in India" initiative, the share of merchandise trade will increase whereas our ports would not have caught up. Against a share of nine percent of railways and six percent of roads in the GDP, the share of ports is only one percent, leading to high logistics costs and making Indian exports uncompetitive. This strategy incorporates both aspects of port-led direct and indirect development[21.] Maritime industry is one of RoKs strengths, paving way for convergence with India's requirements with Sagarmala. This could infuse some energy into Indo RoK trade.

The Emerging Areas -Make in India and RoK. One of the major development drives of the new Government in India is 'Make in India', which intends to transform India into a manufacturing hub. This is a strategy that Hyundai has practised to its benefit. It is also time to scale this relation up to the strategic areas of defence, space and nuclear energy, since they will add value to relations. India has shifted from outright purchase of defence equipment to manufacturing them in India in line with the 'Make in India' policy. This is an inevitable move for any developing country that has a very large defence outflow, with domestic industry that needs orders. Indigenous industry has to eventually absorb technologies and the carry out production in India. It must be seen as an opportunity, since shifting part of the value chain to India can reduce overall costs, making Korean products more competitive in a global market. India can become the proverbial bridge in the business between RoK and other emerging markets. The recent joint statement has indicated RoK as a privileged partner in 'Make in India' plan by Prime Minister Modi. A special vehicle to look at synergising Korean potential in Make in India called the '*Korea Plus*', has also been announced. Ambassador Skand Tayal, highlights that the moot issue in this area is that Korean companies are hesitant for partnerships and desire full control of ventures considering the differences in business cultures. He states further that 'government should offer to lease a shipyard to the Koreans for the long-term on negotiated terms. Such a move would attract the Koreans to not only invest in shipbuilding in India but also bring in modern technology and equipment.' [22] Perhaps, the answer lies in this 'middle path'.

Emerging Areas- Strategic Industries. Two areas to scale up quality in the current content of the commercial relations are space and nuclear cooperation.

- **Space Technology.** India has certain key strengths in space technology, especially in the launch vehicles. Indian Space Research Organisation (ISRO) and the Korea Aerospace Research Institute (KARI) need to pursue cooperation in the areas of lunar exploration where India will share data collected by Chandrayan–1, which was India's lunar mission. Collaboration, interoperability and sharing experience in GAGAN (GPS Aided Geo Augmented Navigation system) and KASS (Korea Augmentation Satellite System) are on the anvil. Deep space cross tracking and communication support for Korean and Indian deep space missions are another emerging area of cooperation in the strategic space domain.

- **Nuclear Energy.** India has a long term plan in place for nuclear energy, eventually leading through the three stage, thorium based reactors. With the nuclear deal, Indian markets have opened up to countries with reactor technology. US, Russia and France are the current leaders, whereas, RoK has immense potential in this domain. India and RoK signed a civil nuclear cooperation agreement in 2011[23]. Present Indian focus is to complete the projects in hand after which, opportunities will open up for RoK in the nuclear energy sector in India.

Learning From Korea. RoK is widely seen in India as a successful model of growth especially in the mannerit reinvented itself as a highly skilled society. PM Modi has been unequivocal about Indian admiration for Korean Growth Story, which any developing nation would like to emulate. India sees Korea as an example in transforming its society through enterprise and industry. With 'Make in India', India will be looking at Korea more intensely, for investments and as model for growth. Amb Tayal has listed certain specific lessons from the Korean model of growth for India. This includes, *'study the Korean experience of rapid skill development producing trained and dedicated manpower in the 1960s and 1970s which caused the impressive industrial miracle of South Korea. The system of vocational training, technical education as well as Research and Development is driven by the requirements of industry. In these areas, India's efforts are largely government-driven and practically divorced from industry requirements. .....3.4 per cent of Korean GDP is spent on research and innovation and 70 per cent of this amount comes from industry!'* [24] India has implemented part of this with the '**Skill India**' program[25] with projects that aims to train over 400 million Indians in different skills by 2022.

Strategic Partnership

Shift in Relations- Upgrade to Higher Level. Taking cue from deepening ties, both countries established 'Long-term Cooperative Partnership for Peace and Prosperity' in 2004. The two countries also started an annual Foreign Policy and Security Dialogue to deliberate on regional and international security issues. Subsequently, the two countries laid the foundation for defence cooperation, by signing a MOU on cooperation in defence industry and logistics in 2005 and another MOU on cooperation between the coast guards of the two countries in 2006. The real turning point in bilateral relations came in the year 2010, when Korea and India upgraded their relationship to a 'Strategic Partnership'. The foundations for a new level of relations- to that of Special Strategic Partnership was laid in January 2014 during President Park's State Visit to India where the leaders agreed to upgrade the bilateral relationship to a 'Special Strategic Partnership'. PM Modi's visit has reaffirmed the process. Democratic values, liberal social and economic order were the basis of this partnership. What is new or special in this architecture is that it includes foreign affairs, defence along with trade and investment, science and technology, culture and people-to-people exchanges and regional cooperation to take the bilateral relations to a qualitatively higher level[26]. As per the new degree of partnership, India and RoK will have a diplomatic and security dialogue in a 2+2 format where, both defence and foreign secretaries will hold joint talks together annually. This gives an opportunity to address security affairs in a far more comprehensive manner. The National Security Councils of both countries will also interact with each other. The joint statement also indicated cooperation for Cyber security and terrorism. There will be greater interaction between the National Defence College of India and the National Defence University of Korea. Navies will conduct staff level talks with regular exchanges of visits.

Possibilities of an Asian Quadrangle. To fully grasp potential of India RoK relations, with Asian Architecture in the backdrop, there is a requirement to understand the unique inter relations that the top four economic powers in Asia, i.e. China, Japan, Korea and India share. China and Korea share a cordial relationship whereas, both China as well as Korea do not share a good relation with neighbouring Japan due to historical reasons. India has a difficult relation with neighbouring China, but shares a cordial relationship with RoK and Japan. With cordial relationship with at least two countries in the quadrangle both India and Korea are in a unique position with multiple options to drive the relations in Asia. Both RoK and India are rising powers which can be classified as 'Middle Powers' to use a familiar Korean expression. The bonds between India and RoK are founded on strong tenets without any baggage of history or geography. These special positions must be optimally used to shape Asian relations positively.

India, Korea and Asia. There is a greater understanding in India of the value of RoK as an important partner in its "Act East" policy, and its contribution to bringing peace, stability and security in the Asia Pacific Region. Be it the mature approach to problems in neighbourhood, or the Northeast Asia Peace and Cooperation Initiative (NAPCI), which has *trustpolitik* as the new watchword. The efforts of RoK to bring 'trust' back on the high table through President Park's trust politik is a very refreshing step to humanise international politics where real politik rules. There is a requirement to examine complementarity between NAPCI and Act East Policy in a granular manner to achieve shared goals. One outcome that has been on the anvil is the Korea-Japan-India trilateral. As the Centre of Gravity of the world is shifting to Asia, there is a greater focus on weak security architectures in Asia, despite thriving economies and trade- which has been termed the Asian Paradox. The security scenario is largely driven by US and recently the narrative has shifted to rise of China. The cooperation and competition between US and China has resulted in competing economic and strategic constructs such as TPP, RCEP and OBOR. China has also initiated the China Japan Korea free trade area of which the China-Korea FTA has been signed in Jun 15 [27.] This is a work in progress, with deep potential, considering the economic heft of this trio. On the other hand, US has initiated the Trans Pacific Partnership as well as a mini lateral with its two allies, Korea and Japan. Rajaram Panda, an Indian strategic scholar has argued a case for India Japan RoK trilateral, which is devoid of heavyweights of China and the US. This idea finds traction in India and is endorsed by eminent scholars of Indo Korean relations like Amb Skand Tayal[28.] This paper endorses the view that all three nations must proactively pursue the trilateral. The special strategic relation shared by India with both Japan and Korea is a step in the right direction. Asian relations should not once again in history reflect the bipolarity of cold war.

Indian position on Korean Peninsula. There is an understanding in India of the importance of peace and stability on the Korean peninsula and the role that RoK plays in that area. Since there are parallels in the Indian subcontinent, managing difficult neighbourhood is well understood by both nations. There is common concern over the development of DPRK's nuclear weapons and ballistic missile programs, which is in violation of its international obligations and commitments. India and RoK have jointly urged the DPRK to fully comply with all of its international obligations, including under the relevant UN Security Council resolutions, and to fulfil its commitments under the 2005 Joint Statement of the Six-Party Talks. India has expressed support for RoK's efforts to build trust in the Korean peninsula and to lay the groundwork for peaceful reunification of the Korean peninsula. There is also a shared interest in strengthening global non-proliferation objectives. RoK and India have committed to the eradication of terrorism in   all its forms and manifestations calling for an early conclusion of negotiations on the Comprehensive Convention on International Terrorism. There is common recognition of the need to eliminate terrorist safe havens, infrastructure, terrorist networks and their financing, and stop cross-border movement of terrorists. There is also a shared understanding of the states that play a role in terrorism, which needs to be taken forward.

Conclusion

India- RoK relations has very few parallels, considering the degree and substance it has attained in a short time. History has favoured this relation with several synergies between these nations. Not only have the growth stories and mile stones deepened congruencies, the pattern and timelines of growth offered both nations high complementariness. India's demographics and geographic location aids India-RoK commercial relations as RoK's bridge to emerging markets. People to people contacts have been positive considering Buddhism, cultural impact of Korean Wave and high dependence of Korean white goods in India. The geopolitical factors that limited engagements between both nations during the cold war politics have dissipated long ago. The stage is now set for both countries to seize the opportunity for letting the special strategic partnership flourish. As two significant middle powers, RoK and India relations are destined to play a major role in Asia, as 'engaged democracies' and 'complimentary economies'.

Endnotes

1   "Tagore Fired Korean Imagination 81 Years Ago," *Deccan Herald*, accessed July 22, 2015, http://www.deccanherald.com/content/179106/tagore-fired-korean-imagination-81.html.

2   "Welcome to Embassy of India, Seoul, South Korea," accessed July 22, 2015, http://www.indembassy.or.kr/pages.php?id=21.

3   Stanley Sandler, *The Korean War: An Encyclopedia* (Routledge, 2014), p 146.

4   Stanley Sandler, *The Korean War: An Encyclopedia* (Routledge, 2014).

5   "Six Decades On, Koreans Return the Favour | Latest News & Updates at Daily News & Analysis," *Dna*, accessed July 24, 2015, http://www.dnaindia.com/sport/report-six-decades-on-koreans-return-the-favour-2021595.

6   Robert Barnes, *The US, the UN and the Korean War: Communism in the Far East and the American Struggle for Hegemony in the Cold War* (I.B.Tauris, 2014).

7   Paul M. Edwards, *Historical Dictionary of the Korean War* (Scarecrow Press, 2010).

8   , Skand R. Tayal, *India and the Republic of Korea: Engaged Democracies* (Taylor & Francis Group, 2014), p 77.

9   IANS, "South Korea Looking to Correct Trade Imbalance with India: Envoy," *Business Standard India*, August 31, 2014, http://www.business-standard.com/article/news-ians/south-korea-looking-to-correct-trade-imbalance-with-india-envoy-114083100128_1.html.

10 "Manipur: A Part of India Where Korea Rules - Al Jazeera English," accessed July 25, 2015, http://www.aljazeera.com/indepth/features/2014/02/part-india-where-korea-rules-20142177748733701.html.

11 "PSYchedelic to SS501," *Times Of India Blogs*, accessed July 28, 2015, http://blogs.timesofindia.indiatimes.com/tracking-indian-communities/psychedelic-to-ss501/.

12 "A Little Bit of Korea in Chennai - Livemint," accessed July 25, 2015, http://www.livemint.com/Politics/rmbtf0t81y6HoVSm08XXRJ/A-little-bit-of-Korea-in-Chennai.html.

13 "Learning Skills from Seoul," *The Hindu*, May 18, 2015, http://www.thehindu.com/opinion/op-ed/learning-skills-from-seoul/article7216726.ece.

14 IANS, "South Korea Looking to Correct Trade Imbalance with India."

15 Ibid.

16 "India-South Korea Relations Under the New Modi Government," *The Diplomat*, accessed July 14, 2015, http://thediplomat.com/2014/08/india-south-korea-relations-under-the-new-modi-government/.

17 ibid

18 "India And South Korea Relations: Past And Future Trends - Analysis," *Eurasia Review*, accessed July 14, 2015, http://www.eurasiareview.com/07102012-india-and-south-korea-relations-past-and-future-trends-analysis/.

19 "Who Will Pay for Asia's $8 Trillion Infrastructure Gap? | Asian Development Bank," accessed August 5, 2015, http://www.adb.org/news/infographics/who-will-pay-asias-8-trillion-infrastructure-gap.

20 "Sagarmala: Concept and Implementation towards Blue Revolution," accessed August 20, 2015, http://pmindia.gov.in/en/news_updates/sagarmala-concept-and-implementation-towards-blue-revolution/.

21 Ibid.

22 Ibid.

23 "South Korea Keen on Setting up Nuclear Power Plant in India," *The Hindu*, January 12, 2014, http://www.thehindu.com/news/national/south-korea-keen-on-setting-up-nuclear-power-plant-in-india/article5570162.ece.

24 "Learning Skills from Seoul."

25 "PM Modi Launches Skill India Initiative That Aims to Train 40 Crore People," *NDTV.com*, accessed July 25, 2015, http://www.ndtv.com/india-news/pm-modi-launches-skill-india-initiative-that-aims-to-train-40-crore-people-781897.

26 "'Consider Korea a Crucial Partner in India's Economic Modernisation', Says PM Modi in Seoul: Highlights," *NDTV.com*, accessed July 19, 2015, http://www.ndtv.com/india-news/consider-korea-a-crucial-partner-in-indias-economic-modernisation-says-pm-modi-in-seoul-highlights-764013.

27 "It's Official: China, South Korea Sign Free Trade Agreement," *The Diplomat*, accessed August 24, 2015, http://thediplomat.com/2015/06/its-official-china-south-korea-sign-free-trade-agreement/.

28 Skand R. Tayal, *India and the Republic of Korea: Engaged Democracies* (Taylor & Francis Group, 2014).

Conclusion

– *USI*

India-South Korea bilateral relations achieved a critical landmark with the upgrade of a fast growing relationship to a '*Special Strategic Partnership*'. As a timely initiative intended to contribute to the process of this upgrade, two premier strategic think tanks, namely the United Service Institution of India (USI) and RINSA, Korea National Defence University (KNDU) undertook a joint research project. The project brought together in house security scholars from the Indian and South Korean think tanks to reflect on specified security themes. In true bilateral spirit, a total of eight scholars - four each from USI and KNDU, took part in this project. Since both nations today stand at the cusp of a *special strategic partnership*, four themes of strategic significance were chosen for joint research. The themes broadly dealt with Geopolitics of the Regions, India-South Korea Bilateral Relations, Security Cooperation and Nuclear Issues. Each theme was addressed by two scholars-one from India and one from South Korea. This ensured that each theme was 'viewed' from both vantage spots. The method of research also involved presentation of papers at both institutes. This facilitated cross pollination of ideas and exposure to each other's environment to make the research more meaningful. The scholars involved in this project ranged from academicians, security analysts, experts in nuclear technology to practitioners from field with wide experience of strategy and military diplomacy.

The result has been a bouquet of eight papers that offers multiple perspectives which can be of value to a scholar or a policy maker. Every capital, it is said, views the world around it through its own unique strategic prism. Seoul and New Delhi are not immune to this phenomenon. Even after considering a scholar's individual expertise, approaches and interpretations, respective national narratives have seeped into these papers in adequate measure. Therefore, as a desirable outcome of the exercise, papers bring out what occupies central position in either nation's strategic outlook to a host of issues that has a bearing on strategic choices. Understanding central concerns of Seoul and New Delhi is extremely significant to either side.

In the geopolitical perspective offered by both Indian and Korean scholars, the most significant themes have been the Rise of China and the Rebalance by the USA. The impact of these geopolitical developments on Korean peninsula has been pervasive in Seoul's perspective. The immediate concerns of both nations lay in their neighbourhood. South Korean concerns pivoted around East Asia whereas Indian concerns evolved from a rising China and its nexus with Pakistan. However both nations recognized emergence of the Indo Pacific as a new strategic and economic system, which if disturbed can have far reaching impacts on the entire region. Delhi's perspective reflected the rise of China and US rebalance, albeit, slightly differently from South Korea. Delhi's view of China's rise was with greater concern than Seoul's. Probably, this is an outcome of how both countries have shaped their respective bilateral relations with China, which in turn shares notably unique relations with their respective, troublesome neighbours, North Korea and Pakistan. South Korea views China as a major factor in an eventual peaceful reunification of Korean Peninsula and acts accordingly. For India, China is a rising neighbour with whom it shares an unsettled border which has consistently used Pakistan as a proxy against India. Despite fairly large difference in their USA relations, perspectives on US rebalance were only mildly different. State sponsored terrorism, through non-state actors is a major and live issue in the Indian narrative, whereas nuclear issues and rising nationalism which are presently the primary concerns in East Asia influence the South Korean narrative.

In the nuclear theme the concerns raised by both nations were along expected lines, North Korea and Pakistan expectedly being central to either paper. There is also a shared understanding of the North Korea-Pakistan Nuclear cooperation. Role of China in nuclearizing respective neighborhoods have been reckoned by scholars from both sides. Even within the nuclear theme, academic approaches by scholars offer diversity. If one paper focused on strategic perspectives, the other gave technical details, however; there were similarities too, and significant estimates about the nuclear programs of North Korea and Pakistan was enunciated by the authors .They also highlight the perils of proliferation. Together they offer the policy maker multiple perspectives for taking cognizant decisions and would enrich any student of 'Nuclear Strategy'.

In the section for Security Cooperation, the South Korean scholar argues that distrusts and disputes have been a major challenge to multilateral cooperation in East Asia. It recommends building multilateral cooperation system among states in *Six Party Talks* as a guarantor of successful negotiations. It also states that the participation of third-party neutral countries like India would promote the success of the negotiations. The Indian Scholar has approached the subject highlighting evolving concepts of security and places greater thrust on the bilateral relations. It also offers insights into how India South Korea relations have emerged with uncanny parallels from inception till now and where defence cooperation has the potential to become a driver.

A significant segment of this joint research has been the study of the bilateral relations between India and South Korea. Whilst the Korean Paper highlights significance of bilateral relations within in a larger academic framework of International Relations theory, the Indian paper follows a linear narrative that traces the growth trajectories identifying complementarities to focus on current and future drivers of growth. It is evident from this section that India- South Korea bilateral relations have achieved a unique momentum in a short span of time. This has been facilitated by synchronous growth trajectories of both nations, and entrepreneurial industries which capitalized on opportunities as they emerged. Just as India opened up its market through liberalization in early 1990s, South Korean industries took the risk to invest in India both as a market as well as a production center to leapfrog to other emerging markets. It identifies trade and commerce as the prime driver of relations and articulates defence, space, maritime and nuclear industries as the next drivers of growth highlighting complementarities in those areas. It cautions that if the trade deficits widen or uneven trade policies are unaddressed they could act as a spoiler in economic relations which is a 'driver' in bilateral relations. This section also indicates that politically, the focus must be on identifying what overlaps and what can synergize India's Act East policy with Korea's Northeast Asia Peace and Cooperation Initiative (NAPCI) which are the core foreign policy initiatives to be capitalized.

India- South Korea relationship has very few parallels, considering the degree and substance it has attained in a short time. Not only have the growth stories and mile stones have had deep congruencies, the pattern and timelines of growth offered both nations high complementariness. India's demographics and geographic location aids India-South Korea commercial relations as South Korea's bridge to emerging markets. People to people contacts have been positive considering Buddhism, cultural impact of Korean Wave and high dependence of Korean white goods in India. The geopolitical factors that limited engagements between both nations during the cold war politics have dissipated long ago. The stage is now set for both countries to seize the opportunity for letting the special strategic partnership flourish. The two significant middle powers South Korea and India relations are destined to play a major role in Asia, as 'engaged democracies' and 'complimentary economies'.

This collection of papers is the first structured attempt to state both Indian and South Korean perspectives on chosen strategic themes. It is by no means comprehensive. The hope is that it will serve as the start point of further engagement and research, and will be able to guide those involved in crafting the trajectory of this strategic partnership.

Index

A

Act East Policy 26, 27, 54, 134

Af-Pak region 24, 33

Air Defence Identification Zones 28

Al-Qaeda 24

Anti-Access Area-Denial 23, 25

Anti-satellite weapons 25

Arabian Sea 28

ASEAN 2, 6, 8, 16, 20, 21, 22, 27, 30, 35, 47, 48, 49, 51, 54

ASEAN Regional Forum 16, 51

Asian Infrastructure Investment Bank (AIIB) 30

Asia-Pacific 2, 6, 8, 10, 16, 18, 24, 26, 47, 48, 49, 50, 119, 121

Asia-Pacific Economic Cooperation 16

Assassin's Mace 25

B

Ballistic Missile Defence programs (BMD) 97

Bangladesh- China-India Myanmar 28

Belt and Road Strategy 25

Boko Haram 33

BRICS 34

C

Civilian Nuclear Power Plants 85

Cold War vii, 2, 5, 16, 17, 18, 42, 43, 44, 51, 53, 85, 96, 106, 109, 136

Comprehensive Economic Partnership Agreement (CEPA) 116

Conference on Interaction and Confidence-Building Measures in Asia 25

Conference on Security and Cooperation in Europe (CSCE) 39, 41

Confidence Building Measures (CBMs) 9

Convention on Physical Protection of Nuclear Materials (CPPNM) 97

Council for Security Cooperation in the Asia Pacific 16

Cyber-security 9

D

Defence Acquisition Programme Administration (DAPA 116

Defence Procurement Procedure (DPP) 61

Defence Strategic Guidance (DSG) 8

Diego Garcia 23, 28

Dirty Bombs 95

E

East Asia Summit 2, 16, 34, 51

East China Sea 6, 25

F

Fissile Material Cut-off Treaty (FMCT) 98

Foreign Policy and Security Dialogue (FPSD) 116

Free Trade Agreement (FTA) 30

G

General Security of Military Information Agreement (GSOMIA) 116

Global Initiative to Combat Nuclear Terrorism (GICNT) 98

Global Nuclear Disarmament 87

GPS Aided Geo-Augmented Navigation System (GAGAN) 62, 131

H

Hamas 29, 33

Hezbollah 29

Highly Enriched Uranium (HEU) 69, 72, 76, 89

Hu Jintao 7, 25

I

Indian Space Research Organisation (ISRO) 131

India's Act East Policy 26

Indo-Pacific v, viii, 1, 2, 3, 17, 21, 22, 23, 29, 35

International Atomic Energy Agency (IAEA) 87, 98

International Convention for the Suppression of Acts of Nuclear Terrorism (ICSANT) 98

International Institute of Strategic Studies (IISS) 31

K

Kangnam Corporation 60

Khunjerab pass 28

Korea Aerospace Research Institute (KARI) 131

Korea Augmentation Satellite System (KASS) 62, 131

Korean Central News Agency (KCNA) 71

Kurile Islands 28

L

Look East Policy 2, 54

M

Multilateral Security Cooperation 37, 39, 42, 48, 50

N

Neutral Nations Repatriation Committee (NNRC) 124

New Development Bank (NDB) 30

Non-state actors 14, 15, 19, 33, 52, 86, 90, 95, 99, 139

North American Aerospace Defence (NORAD) 79

North Atlantic Treaty Organization (NATO) 41

Northeast Asian Peace and Cooperation Initiative 17

Nuclear Non-Proliferation Treaty (NPT) 72, 87

O

ONGC Videsh Limited 58

Organization for Security and Cooperation in Europe (OSCE) 37, 38, 39, 41, 43, 45

P

Pacific Ocean 21, 23, 25, 26

Pakistan Occupied Kashmir (POK) 29

Pan-Asian Free Trade Area 27

Paracel islands 27

Persian Gulf 28

R

Radiological Dispersal Device 95

Regional Comprehensive Economic Partnership (RCEP) 30

Republic of Korea (ROK) 51

Research Institute for National Security Affairs (RINSA) vii

Russia's Pivot to East Asia 26

S

Scud-B missiles 70

Sea lines of communication 25, 27, 28, 29, 56

Senkaku/Diaoyu islands 10, 22

Shangri-La Dialogue 16, 24

Silk Road Economic Belt 25

Six Party Talks 16, 47, 135, 140

South China Sea 5, 6, 8, 9, 10, 12, 24

Special Strategic Partnership 56

Spratly Islands 27

Strait of Lambok 21

Strait of Malacca 21

Strait of Sunda 21

T

Tactical Nuclear Weapons (TNWs) 32,
   88, 90, 91

Trans-Pacific Partnership (TPP) 30

W

Wahabi-Salafi ideology 33

Weapons of Mass Destruction (WMD)
   33, 57, 59, 64, 69

X

Xi Jinping 7, 18, 20, 25

Y

Yeonpyeong Island 57

www.ingramcontent.com/pod-product-compliance
Lightning Source LLC
Chambersburg PA
CBHW021537260326
41914CB00001B/52